Depression and Families: Impact and Treatment

Series

David Spiegel, M.D.,
Series Editor

Depression and Families: Impact and Treatment

Edited by
Gabor I. Keitner, M.D.

1400 K Street, N.W.
Washington, DC 20005

Note: The authors have worked to ensure that all information in this book concerning drug dosages, schedules, and routes of administration is accurate as of the time of publication and consistent with standards set by the U.S. Food and Drug Administration and the general medical community. As medical research and practice advance, however, therapeutic standards may change. For this reason and because human and mechanical errors sometimes occur, we recommend that readers follow the advice of a physician who is directly involved in their care or the care of a member of their family.

Manufactured in the United States of America
First Edition 92 91 90 89 5 4 3 2 1

The paper used in this publication meets the minimum requirements of the American National Standard for Information Sciences—Permanence of Paper for Printed Library Materials, ANSI Z39.48-1984.

Library of Congress Cataloging-in-Publication Data

Depression and families: impact and treatment/edited by Gabor I. Keitner.—1st ed.
p. cm.—(The Progress in psychiatry series)
Includes bibliographies.
ISBN 0-88048-223-0 (alk. paper)
1. Depression, Mental—Patients—Family relationships. 2. Parent and child. 3. Psychotherapy. I. Keitner, Gabor I., 1947- .
II. Series.
[DNLM: 1. Depressive Disorder. 2. Family. 3. Family Therapy. 4. Interpersonal Relations. WM 171 D42245]
RC537.D42744 1989
616.85'27—dc20
DNLM/DLC
for Library of Congress 89-15117
CIP

For my children,
Chimène and Haydon

Contents

Contributors

Carol M. Anderson, Ph.D.
Professor of Psychiatry, University of Pittsburgh School of Medicine, Associate Administrator, Western Psychiatric Institute, Pittsburgh, Pennsylvania

William R. Beardslee, M.D.
Associate Professor of Psychiatry, Harvard Medical School, Clinical Director, The Children's Hospital, Boston, Massachusetts

Duane S. Bishop, M.D.
Associate Professor of Psychiatry, Brown University Program in Medicine, Director of Rehabilitation, Rhode Island Hospital, Providence, Rhode Island

John F. Clarkin, Ph.D.
Professor of Clinical Psychology in Psychiatry, Cornell University Medical College, New York, New York

Sandra J. Coffman, Ph.D.
Psychologist, Seattle, Washington

James C. Coyne, Ph.D.
Associate Professor, Department of Psychiatry, University of Michigan Medical School, Ann Arbor, Michigan

Nathan B. Epstein, M.D.
Professor Emeritus, Brown University Program in Medicine, Providence, Rhode Island, Physician-in-Chief, Parkwood Hospital, New Bedford, Massachusetts

Ira D. Glick, M.D.
Professor of Psychiatry, Cornell University Medical College, New York, New York

Gretchen L. Haas, Ph.D.
Assistant Professor of Psychology in Psychiatry, Cornell University Medical College, New York, New York

Diane Holder, M.S.W.
Assistant Professor of Psychiatry, University of Pittsburgh School of Medicine, Associate Director, Center for Children and Families, Pittsburgh, Pennsylvania

Jill M. Hooley, D.Phil.
Assistant Professor of Psychology, Harvard University, Boston, Massachusetts

Neil S. Jacobson, Ph.D.
Professor and Director, Clinical Psychology Program, University of Washington, Seattle, Washington

Gabor I. Keitner, M.D.
Associate Professor of Psychiatry, Brown University Program in Medicine, Director, Affective Disorders Program, Butler Hospital, Providence, Rhode Island

Kathleen R. Merikangas, Ph.D.
Assistant Professor of Psychiatry and Epidemiology, Yale University School of Medicine, New Haven, Connecticut

Ivan W. Miller, Ph.D.
Associate Professor of Psychiatry, Brown University Program in Medicine, Director, Family Research, Butler Hospital, Providence, Rhode Island

Brigitte A. Prusoff, Ph.D.
Research Scientist, Department of Psychiatry, Yale University School of Medicine, New Haven, Connecticut

James H. Spencer, Jr., M.D.
Clinical Associate Professor of Psychiatry, Cornell University Medical College, New York, New York

Myrna M. Weissman, Ph.D.
Professor of Epidemiology in Psychiatry, College of Physicians and Surgeons, Columbia University, New York, New York

Introduction to the Progress in Psychiatry Series

The *Progress in Psychiatry* Series is designed to capture in print the excitement that comes from assembling a diverse group of experts from various locations to examine in detail the newest information about a developing aspect of psychiatry. This series emerged as a collaboration between the American Psychiatric Association's Scientific Program Committee and the American Psychiatric Press, Inc. Great interest was generated by a number of the symposia presented each year at the APA Annual Meeting, and we realized that much of the information presented there, carefully assembled by people who are deeply immersed in a given area, would unfortunately not appear together in print. The symposia sessions at the Annual Meetings provide an unusual opportunity for experts who otherwise might not meet on the same platform to share their diverse viewpoints for a period of three hours. Some new themes are repeatedly reinforced and gain credence, while in other instances disagreements emerge, enabling the audience and now the reader to reach informed decisions about new directions in the field. The *Progress in Psychiatry* Series allows us to publish and capture some of the best of the symposia and thus provide an in-depth treatment of specific areas which might not otherwise be presented in broader review formats.

Psychiatry is by nature an interface discipline, combining the study of mind and brain, of individual and social environments, of the humane and the scientific. Therefore, progress in the field is rarely linear—it often comes from unexpected sources. Further, new developments emerge from an array of viewpoints that do not necessarily provide immediate agreement but rather expert examination of the issues. We intend to present innovative ideas and data that will enable you, the reader, to participate in this process.

We believe the *Progress in Psychiatry* Series will provide you with an opportunity to review timely new information in specific fields of interest as they are developing. We hope you find that the excitement of the presentations is captured in the written word and that this book proves to be informative and enjoyable reading.

David Spiegel, M.D.
Series Editor
Progress in Psychiatry Series

Introduction

It is time for an overview of our current understanding of the impact of depressive illness on the families of depressed persons, as well as the influence of family functioning on the course of the depression. Research over the past decade has made it increasingly clear that major depression, like any other illness, does not exist or evolve in a vacuum, but is intrinsically bound to a social context, most immediately the family. Living with a depressed person is difficult, demanding, and at times overwhelming. In turn, the ways in which families are able to deal with this burden and their particular pattern of relationships and interactional styles appear to have a significant impact on the course of the depressive illness itself.

Much has been postulated about the neurochemical and neurophysiological underpinnings of major depression. Less attention has been paid to its social context. Yet, clearly, the two are not separable. Although we are far from being able to describe the precise mechanisms involved in this interplay between biology and its psychosocial context, evidence of its importance for the understanding and treatment of major depression is mounting. This book brings together current findings and conceptual overviews in this area from leading research groups. This volume is divided into three sections: the first section reviews what we know about the interplay between depression and family functioning, the second section addresses the impact of depression on children and adolescents in these families, and the final section outlines a variety of treatment approaches that involve the family.

Our study, from the Brown/Butler family research program, identifies the impact of depression on the family during the acute phase of the episode, discusses what happens to the family as the episode remits, and looks at the interesting question of the course of depressive illness as related to changes within the family. This study provides data emphasizing the importance of recognizing and addressing family issues in depressed patients in order to ensure optimum treatment for the depressive episode itself. Dr. Coyne presents a review and an overview of the interpersonal processes that are a part of the depressed person's social/familial interactions. He attempts to elucidate on a more behavioral and molecular level the specific patterns of interactions that are problematic for depressed patients and their families. Dr. Hooley provides an excellent overview of the expressed emotion (EE) concept, as well as a detailed description of its relevance to depressed patients, showing again that depressed patients seem even more sensitive to criticism than patients with schizophrenia. She also presents fascinating new data on sequential analyses of interactions in high- and low-EE couples in order to understand better the dynamics of these interactions.

Of major social and clinical concern is what happens to the children of depressed parents. What data are available to enable us to advise families about risks to their offspring and to suggest early interventions? Dr. Merikangas and her colleagues discuss the high rate of impairment (33–45%) in these children. They present sobering data on the problems for children when both parents have diagnosable psychiatric disorders. The issue of assortative mating is one that is likely to assume increasing significance in the family field. Dr. Beardslee also emphasizes that children, especially adolescents, of depressed parents are at high risk of having an affective episode themselves. He provides an unusual and refreshing perspective by first focusing on a subgroup of youngsters who have shown themselves to be resilient to the effects of their parents' illness and then uses knowledge gained from them to outline a preventive intervention program for families with depressed members.

The third section of the book deals with the practical issues of treatment of families with depressed members, building on groundwork laid out in the earlier chapters. Unfortunately, sound empirical evidence for the effectiveness of family interventions in these families, in terms of shortening the depressive episode, reducing the risk of relapse, or impacting on the family's ability to cope with the illness, is not yet available. Such studies are sorely needed. Dr. Clarkin and his colleagues present data from the only currently available controlled study of family intervention for hospitalized patients with affective disorders. Their work is an important first step in bringing greater empirical rigor into the family therapy field. Common sense, clinical intuition, and everyday practice strongly suggest that family approaches may be helpful. Two types of family treatments are presented in some detail. Dr. Coffman and Dr. Jacobson describe a social-learning–based model of family therapy, providing a detailed clinical description of one couple, that allows a closer look at what actually is done with this model in each treatment session. Along similar lines, Ms. Holder and Dr. Anderson provide a practical guide for the use of psychoeducational groups (a model that has made a significant impact on the treatment of schizophrenia) to help depressed patients and their families cope with the depressive illness. They discuss the use of this model in families in which the patient has a child or an elderly family member.

In reading these chapters, a note of caution is advised. Affective disorders are a heterogeneous group of illnesses with a broad range of symptoms and symptom severity. Some patients are dysphoric but quite functional, whereas others are profoundly depressed and in need of hospitalization. Before attempting to apply the information contributed to this volume, it is important to establish the specific population—inpatient or outpatient, dysthymic or those with major depression—from which the data derive and for whom the treatment is intended. Too often it is erroneously assumed that the same issues are applicable to all forms of affective illness.

Even with these cautionary notes in mind, there is a clear and consistent theme in the chapters of this book. Depression in all its varied presentations is a serious illness with significant consequences for the patient and his or her family. By recognizing this reality, clinicians can target their interventions more effectively to include both the patient and the family members. More broadly, this book will hopefully provide a further impetus to more comprehensive psychosocial treatments for patients with depression.

I would like to express my thanks and acknowledge my indebtedness to my secretary, Mrs. Tanya Baur, for her tireless efforts in the preparation of this book.

Gabor I. Keitner, M.D.

Chapter 1

Family Processes and the Course of Depressive Illness

Gabor I. Keitner, M.D.
Ivan W. Miller, Ph.D.
Nathan B. Epstein, M.D.
Duane S. Bishop, M.D.

Chapter 1

Family Processes and the Course of Depressive Illness

Depression is a major burden for both depressed patients and their family members. The extent and nature of this burden has increasingly become the focus of recent studies. There are many reasons for this emerging interest in the families of depressed patients. Interest in affective illness, and depression in particular, has grown with the development of clearer diagnostic criteria in DSM-III (1980), the availability of effective pharmacologic agents for its treatment, and viable neurochemical theories of its etiology. Paradoxically, the expectations raised by this recent biological perspective, with its promise of ready cures via pharmacologic management of the depressive episodes, have led to disillusionment. Psychopharmacologic agents alone are effective with only 50–70% of depressed patients, leaving a substantial proportion of patients who need additional or alternative treatments. Concurrent with the biological approach has been a steady growth of interest in family therapy and family functioning, a trend that is being reinforced by the development of more reliable instruments for measuring family processes. The current interest in families of depressed patients parallels the significant work done with families of schizophrenic patients in the 1950s and 1960s.

This chapter reviews our present understanding of the relationship between family functioning and depression, focusing particularly on the course of the depressive illness. We will summarize what is known about the impact of depression on families during the acute depressive episode, how family functioning changes as the depressive episode remits, and what family factors may contribute to relapse. Particular focus will be on family variables related to the course of the depressive illness through presentation of data from our own recent work. We will also highlight some theoretical issues that, though unresolved, have a significant bearing on our understanding of families and depression. Finally, we will emphasize the clinical implications of our current state of knowledge. We will not address to any great extent the impact of depression on children in these families or review studies assessing the effectiveness of family therapy in this population, as both of these areas are reviewed elsewhere in this volume. In this chapter, we will restrict our observations to patients with major depression, primarily those with symptoms severe enough to require hospitalization.

RELATIONSHIP BETWEEN FAMILY FUNCTIONING AND DEPRESSION

One of the problems in trying to assess the relationship between a relapsing and remitting illness and family processes is that both the illness and the family are changing over time. It is therefore critical to establish defined time frames in which the relationship can be examined, both to obtain a clearer perspective on issues of causality and to allow legitimate comparisons with other studies. The two most logical time frames for such studies are during the acute episode and at the time of remission of symptoms.

Family Functioning During the Acute Depressive Episode

A substantial number of studies document the impact that depression has on the families of depressed patients during the acute depressive episode. Weissman and Paykel (1974), in their seminal study of 40 moderately to severely depressed female outpatients, identified significant problems in the social and family functioning of these women. They found depressed women to be more reticent in their communications, more submissive and dependent, less affectionate toward their spouses, and experiencing more friction and arguments with their husbands than did nondepressed control women. They also experienced more friction with their children and were reluctant to discuss personal feelings. Hinchliffe et al. (1975) observed 20 depressed psychiatric inpatients and their spouses during the acute depressive episode and found a greater level of negative hostile behavior, more self-preoccupation, negative tension (tense, stuttering, and emotionally tinged speech), and more attempts at controlling other people than in nondepressed control couples with one member hospitalized for surgery. These and other earlier studies have been reviewed elsewhere (Keitner et al. 1985).

More recent studies using varied patient populations and assessment procedures have continued to find that families of depressed patients experience significant problems during the most active phase of the illness. These disturbances are evident over a wide range of family functions. Biglan et al. (1985) observed a sample of 27 depressed female outpatients interacting with their families at home. They found that these women displayed less problem-solving behavior than their husbands and that there was less self-disclosure than in nondepressed couples. It was further found (Hops et al. 1987) that depressed mothers' family environments were no more aversive than those of nondepressed mothers, but rather that the depressed women and their families appeared to be locked into an interacting style that promoted high rates of aversive interchanges between family members.

It is not surprising that during the acute phase of an illness the family of the ill patient is upset and feels undue strain when compared with "normal" or control families. Of even greater interest are studies suggesting that depressive illness is associated with a greater degree of family strain and impairment than other psychiatric illnesses and some medical conditions. In our studies, families of patients with major depression consistently showed the most impaired family functioning (75% reported disturbances) when compared with families of patients with alcohol dependence, adjustment disorders, schizophrenia, or bipolar disorder (Miller et al. 1986).

Similarly, Crowther (1985) compared family functioning in 27 inpatients with major depression with family functioning in patients with schizophrenia, bipolar illness, or anxiety disorder or in alcohol-abusing patients. He noted that depressed patients reported significantly more marital maladjustment and desired significantly more changes in their marriages than did the other psychiatric inpatients. These findings were confirmed by the patients' therapists. Bouras et al. (1986), looking at depressed outpatients, found that depression had a much greater impact on marital life from the patients' and the spouses' points of view than did rheumatoid arthritis or cardiac illness.

Family therapists have tended to assume that a noxious family environment is in some way responsible for a patient's symptomatology. However, it is becoming recognized that the patient's illness has a major impact on other family members. Increased attention is being given to the difficulties experienced by family members having to cope on a daily basis with a depressed relative. Coyne et al. (1987) found that over 40% of adults living with a patient in a depressive episode were distressed themselves to the point of meeting criteria for needing therapeutic intervention. Family members found the patient's lack of interest in social life, fatigue, feelings of hopelessness, and constant worrying to be the aspects most disturbing for them. The burden on family members was felt more significantly during the acute episode. Fadden et al. (1987) described the severe burden borne by spouses of depressed patients. They noted in particular that the negative effects of mental illness, rather than the florid symptoms, were the most problematic for family members, who had resisted attributing the patient's worrying, social withdrawal, irritability, and nagging to the mental illness.

Our family research group compared family functioning in families of 43 depressed inpatients with 29 nonpsychiatric control families and found that the families of the depressed patients reported significant dysfunction, particularly in family communications, problem solving, and the capacity of individual family members to experience appropriate affect over a range of stimuli (Keitner et al. 1986).

A subsequent study of depressed inpatients and their families also confirmed the wide range of family functions that are perceived as being problematic. Sixty-four percent of these families felt that their overall functioning was impaired (Keitner et al. 1987a; Figure 1, Table 2).

To understand the specific difficulties that depressed families report during the acute episode, we compared responses to particular items

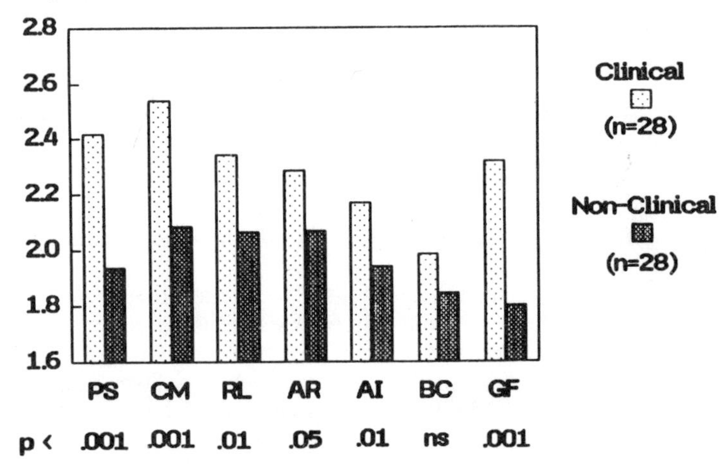

Figure 1. Clinical families (during the acute phase) versus matched nonclinical control families. Reprinted with permission from Keitner et al. 1987a. Copyright 1987 Grune & Stratton, Inc. FAD = Family Assessment Device; PS = problem solving; CM = communication; RL = roles; AR = affective responsiveness; AI = affective involvement; BC = behavior control; GF = general functioning.

on the Family Assessment Device (to be described in detail later in this chapter) from a sample of acutely depressed psychiatric inpatients and their families with responses from nonclinical matched families. The families of the depressed patients complained of difficulties resolving emotional upsets, handling day-to-day problems, acting on decisions, addressing problems, and dealing with problems involving feelings. Families with depressed members also had difficulties talking about tender feelings, being able to express themselves clearly, and not knowing how to discuss issues when they were angry. Families with depressed members also had difficulties with family role issues; they had trouble allocating household tasks and responsibilities and ensuring that family members met their responsibilities and completed duties assigned to them.

Families of the depressed patients felt less able to show love or affection for each other and were concerned about the lack of emotional responsiveness in other family members. They also felt that family members got involved with each other only when they had a personal interest in the matter. This lack of involvement alternated with overinvolvement when a family member was in trouble. There appeared to be difficulty modulating a consistently appropriate affective distance within the family.

Family rules and regulations were also problematic in that families of the depressed patients were unclear about what to do in emergency situations and were not sure what to expect if family rules were broken. They were upset about their inability to discuss their fears and to express their feelings, leading to a general perception that there were many bad feelings within the family.

The majority of these studies using various methodologies and a fairly diverse patient population have consistently shown that during the acute episode, families of patients with major depression experience significant difficulties in many areas of their family life. Communications in the family are particularly problematic, especially appropriate self-disclosure by the depressed patient. Depressed women tend to be aversive to others and exhibit impaired parenting; the families as a whole experience difficulties in their ability to solve problems. Overall, families with depressed members appear to experience more difficulties than do families of patients with schizophrenia or bipolar illness, or families of patients with rheumatoid arthritis or cardiac disease.

Family Functioning at Remission

The finding of family disturbances during the acute depressive episode leads to the following series of questions. Are the difficulties reported during the acute episode a reflection of the family's response to the patient's depression or do they represent a more chronic pattern of family dysfunction? More specifically, does family functioning change after recovery from the acute episode? If so, does family functioning return to a "normal" level? These questions are important in that a search for their answers may shed further light on the interactive process between the illness and the family context in which it takes place.

Rounsaville et al. (1980), looking at the marriages of depressed female outpatients during the acute episode and at a 48-month follow-up, found that although there was some improvement in marital satisfaction as the depressive episode resolved, most depressed women continued to experience greater dissatisfaction in their marriages than nondepressed control women. About half of the marriages that had improved over the course of the resolution of the depressive illness deteriorated by 48 months. They concluded that marriages tend to be either good or disturbed over time. The quality of marriages over the course of the depressive illness and at remission was related more to the quality of the marriage before the onset of the depressive episode than to the depressive illness. Goering et al. (1983) reported that depressed female outpatients continued to experience marital difficulties even as their depression resolved. Merikangas et al. (1985) assessed marital functioning in 45 depressed inpatients at the point of remission from their depression. They reported that, at recovery, depressed couples rated their marriages as significantly worse in all areas than did control couples; there was, in addition, a higher prevalence of serious psychiatric and medical illness in their children.

Hinchliffe et al. (1977) noted that the communication patterns of couples with a depressed member tended to become more like those of control couples as the depressive episode remitted.

Billings and Moos (1985a) reported on a study of 424 depressed inpatients and outpatients assessed during the acute depressive episode and at a 12-month follow-up. Thirty-five percent of the group were found to be remitted, 31% partially remitted, and 34% nonremitted. In addition, remitted patients reported significantly fewer negative events and fewer family arguments at follow-up than during the acute episode. Remitted patients experienced somewhat-reduced stress, although they did not fully reach "normal" levels. The remitted patients also approached, but did not fully reach, the level of social resources (friends, supportive family interactions) observed for a community-matched control group. Billings and Moos (1985b) noted that although the social environments of remitted patients and their families improved, their children were still functioning more poorly than children of a control group. Nonetheless, the family environments of remitted patients were consistently more positive than those of the nonremitted patients.

Dobson (1987) assessed family functioning in two groups of depressed outpatients—those in the acute stage and those remitted—and a control group. He found, consistent with the previously mentioned studies, that marital adjustment was most problematic in the acute stage group and least problematic in the control group, with the remitted group functioning in the middle. He concluded that poor social functioning and marital maladjustment tended to diminish with remission of the depressive symptoms.

Our own work supports these findings. We assessed 28 families of depressed inpatients during the acute episode and at remission of the depressive symptoms (Keitner et al. 1987a). We found that although depressed families did exhibit some improvement in certain areas of family functioning after remission of the depression (Figure 2), they reported significantly poorer functioning than control fam-

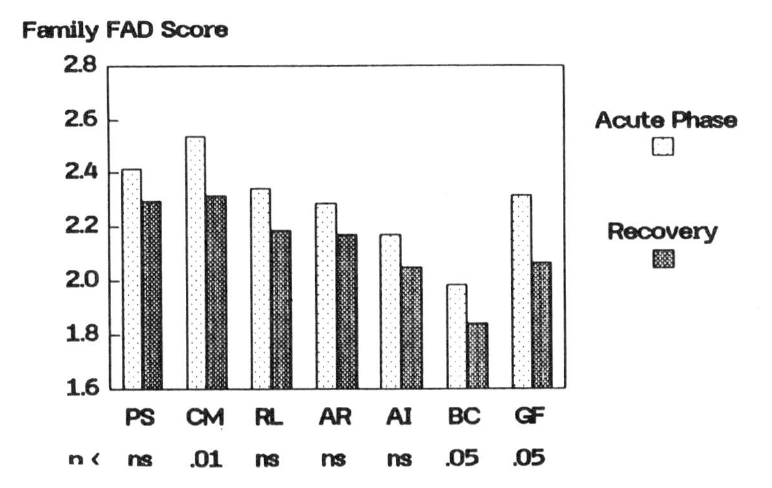

Figure 2. Clinical families at acute phase versus recovery. Reprinted with permission from Keitner et al. 1987a. Copyright 1987 Grune & Stratton, Inc. n = 23 (includes only patients who recovered. FAD = Family Assessment Device; PS = problem solving; CM = communication; RL = roles; AR = affective responsiveness; AI = affective involvement; BC = behavior control; GF = general functioning.

ilies, particularly in their ability to solve problems, to communicate with each other, and to feel generally satisfied with their overall functioning (Figure 3). At remission, 46% of the clinical families still felt that their overall functioning was impaired in contrast to only 18% of the matched nonclinical families. (Table 2).

In general, there is remarkable consistency in the findings of studies that have examined changes in family functioning as the depressive illness remits. With the diminution of depressive symptomatology, although there is improvement in family functioning over time, these families continue to experience more problems than do nonclinical families. It seems evident that continued work with and support for these families is warranted even after the depressive episode has subsided. It is still not clear, however, to what extent the ongoing problems in these families are a function of the depressive illness itself or of other factors. There is evidence that the nature and duration of the family dysfunction may antedate and be independent of the depressive illness, a question that will be addressed later in this discussion.

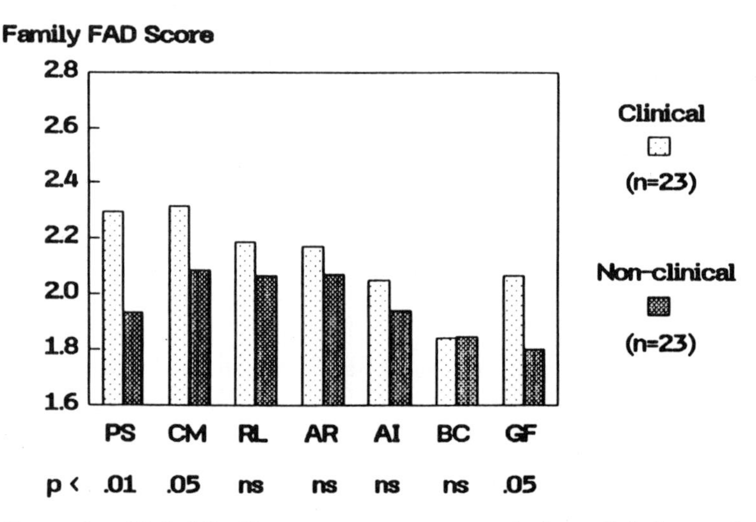

Figure 3. Clinical families at recovery versus matched nonclinical control families. Reprinted with permission from Keitner et al. 1987a. Copyright 1987 Grune & Stratton, Inc. FAD = Family Assessment Device; PS = problem solving; CM = communication; RL = roles; AR = affective responsiveness; AI = affective involvement; BC = behavior control; GF = general functioning.

Family Functioning and the Course of the Depressive Illness

A further important question is the relationship of family functioning to the course of the depressive illness. That is, is family functioning associated with rates of recovery? More specifically, are patients with poor family functioning in the acute phase of the illness more likely to have a slow rate of recovery? Does change in the quality of family life have any bearing on the course of the depressive illness? Very few studies have addressed this issue.

Rounsaville et al. (1979) reported that a reduction in the number of marital disputes was associated with improved depressive symptoms and social functioning after 8 months of individual psychotherapy in depressed female outpatients. Looking at it in another way, Corney (1987) noted that women who had major marital problems were more likely to be depressed at follow-up than those with good relationships. In her study of 80 depressed women patients in general practice, Corney found that the quality of the patient's marital relationship was crucial in affecting clinical outcome. In a 1-month follow-up study of 75 depressed inpatients, Waring and Patton (1984) suggested that the quality of intimacy in a relationship may be predictive of the outcome of the depression—patients still depressed at the follow-up period indicated lower intimacy in their relationships than those who had improved.

In an attempt to further understand the effect of family functioning on the duration of the depressive disorder, we studied 38 psychiatric inpatients and their families (Keitner et al. 1987a). Patients were eligible for this study if they 1) met the DSM-III criteria for unipolar major depression, 2) were currently living with one or more family members, and 3) agreed to participate with their family in the study. A matched sample of control families was drawn from a larger data base of 124 demographically mixed nonclinical families. Control families were matched with depressed families on family stage (i.e., number and ages of children and ages of parents) and socioeconomic status.

Assessment of family functioning. Family functioning was assessed with the Family Assessment Device (FAD) (Epstein et al. 1983), a 60-item self-report questionnaire assessing the six dimensions of the McMaster Model of Family Functioning (Epstein et al. 1978) as well as the family's overall level of functioning (General Functioning).

The psychometric properties of the FAD have been described in previous publications (Epstein et al. 1983; Miller et al. 1985). Briefly, published data suggest that the FAD subscales have 1) adequate internal consistency (.72–.92), 2) adequate test/retest reliability (.66–

.76), and 3) low correlations with social desirability (.06–.19). The FAD has been found to differentiate between families rated as healthy or unhealthy by experienced clinicians for each dimension, as well as to correlate in their expected directions with other self-report measures of family functioning (Miller et al. 1985). Although the correlations between subscales of the FAD are moderate (.37–.67), these correlations are theoretically consistent and approach zero when the effects of General Functioning are covaried (Epstein et al. 1983). The FAD has been used in numerous previous studies, including four previous studies investigating family functioning in families of depressed patients (Keitner et al. 1986, 1987a, 1987b; Miller et al. 1986).

The McMaster model comprises six dimensions of family functioning: 1) *Problem solving* concerns the family's ability to proceed through seven steps from problem identification to problem resolution in both instrumental and affective areas. 2) *Communication* refers to the effectiveness and extent of the family's style of communication. Effective communication is defined as the transmission of clear and direct verbal messages. 3) *Roles* are the recurrent patterns of behavior necessary to fulfill the instrumental and affective needs of family members. Roles responsive to instrumental needs include the provision of essential resources, such as money, shelter, clothing, and food. Affective functions include the provision of nurturing and the development of life skills for both children and parents. Systems maintenance and management functions include rules and decision making, management of finances and health, and maintenance of the family's standards and boundaries. 4) *Affective responsiveness* assesses the ability of family members to respond with the appropriate quality and quantity of feelings to a wide range of stimuli. Both welfare (love, happiness, joy) and emergency (anger, sadness, fear) affects are considered. 5) *Affective involvement* refers to the amount of interest, care, and concern family members invest in each other. For example, "overinvolvement" describes parents who are overly tied up with each other and/or their children, whereas "lack of involvement" applies when family members show only minimal interest and/or concern for each other. Other styles considered are involvement devoid of feelings and empathic, narcissistic, and symbiotic involvement. 6) *Behavioral control* defines the family's style of maintaining discipline and standards of behavior. Standards and latitudes may lead to styles that are rigid, flexible, chaotic, or laissez-faire.

Procedure. The depressed patient and family members over the age of 12 years were administered the FAD during the patient's hospitalization for the depressive episode. After discharge from the hospital, the Modified Hamilton Rating Scale for Depression (Miller et al. 1985) was administered on a monthly basis over the telephone. Patients were followed until their recovery from the depressive episode (Modified Hamilton Rating Scale score less than 9 for 3 consecutive months) or for 12 months if recovery was not achieved. At the end of follow-up (recovery or 12 months), the patient and all family members were again asked to complete FADs. No attempt was made to control treatment during the follow-up period. Outpatients were treated by their own psychiatrists with standard pharmacological and psychotherapeutic techniques. Only two patients and their families had any type of family therapy. Control families were contacted by mail and asked to complete a demographic information form and the FAD.

Twenty-eight patients (21 female, 7 male) and their spouses completed the follow-up. Their ages ranged from 18 to 64, with a mean of 38.0 years (SD = 13.9). There were no differences in family functioning between those who dropped out and those who completed the follow-up (Table 1). The family role of the patients included 18 wives, 6 husbands, and 4 children. Twenty-five of the 28 patients who completed the study were recovered by the 12-month follow-up.

As noted above, the depressed families had worse family func-

Table 1. Demographic data for completers and dropouts

	Completers (n = 28)	Dropouts (n = 10)
Sex		
Male	7	6
Female	21	4
SES (Nock and Rossi 1979)	58.5	56.6
Patient age (years)	38.0	45.5
Family role		
Husband	6	6
Wife	18	4
Child	4	0
Education (years)	13	11
Marital status		
First marriage for both spouses (%)	54	43
Reconstituted (%)	27	57
Divorced, separated, or widowed (%)	19	0

Note. SES = socioeconomic status. Reprinted with permission from Keitner et al. 1987a. Copyright 1987 Grune & Stratton, Inc.

tioning than the control families, both during the acute episode and at the time of recovery.

To investigate the relationship between family functioning during the acute episode and time to recovery, the depressed sample was subdivided into families functioning well or poorly for each FAD dimension, according to their scores on the acute-episode FAD (Table 2). Clinically validated FAD cutoff scores were used for this subdivision (Miller et al. 1985). The time to recovery then was compared for each set of families with depressed members functioning well versus poorly. These analyses yielded no significant results (Table 3). Similarly, correlations between acute-episode FAD scores and time to recovery were low and not significant. There was no significant difference in time to recovery between male and female patients.

Major findings did emerge when families of depressed patients were subdivided into Improvers versus Nonimprovers based on the absolute change between acute and follow-up FAD scores. Patients from families who improved on the general functioning scale had a significantly shorter time to recovery (4.1 months) than patients from families who did not improve (8.1 months) (Table 4). Also, patients from families who improved on the communication, roles, and affective involvement scales showed nonsignificant trends toward hav-

Table 2. Proportion of healthy families, determined by use of clinically established FAD cutoffs

	Acute phase		Follow-up		Nonclinical controls	
	n	%	*n*	%	*n*	%
Problem solving	12**	43	23	82	22	79
Communication	6**	21	11	39	19	68
Roles	13	40	19	68	20	71
Affective responsiveness	11	39	17	61	18	64
Affective involvement	12**	43	16	57	22	79
Behavior control	11	39	16	57	16	57
General functioning	10**	36	15*	54	23	82

Note. $N = 28$. FAD = Family Assessment Device. Reprinted with permission from Keitner et al. 1987a. Copyright 1987 Grune & Stratton, Inc.

*$P < .05$ in comparison with nonclinical control families. **$P < .01$ in comparison with nonclinical control families.

ing a shorter recovery time. Improvement in problem solving and behavior control was not associated with length of time to recovery.

Therefore, although acute-episode family functioning was not associated with speed of recovery, positive changes in overall family functioning during the course of illness were associated with shorter recovery times.

Our findings, then, are consistent with previous studies in suggesting that the quality of the patients' social environment has a considerable impact on the course and duration of the depressive illness.

Table 3. Recovery time by acute-phase FAD, determined by use of established FAD cutoffs

	Healthy families (months)	Unhealthy families (months)
Problem solving	4.8 ± 3.0	5.6 ± 3.6
Communication	5.7 ± 3.7	5.1 ± 3.3
Roles	5.3 ± 3.5	5.2 ± 3.3
Affective responsiveness	4.4 ± 2.9	5.8 ± 3.6
Affective involvement	5.5 ± 3.6	5.1 ± 3.3
Behavior control	3.7 ± 1.6	6.2 ± 5.6
General functioning	4.6 ± 3.1	5.6 ± 3.5

Note. No differences were statistically significant. FAD = Family Assessment Device. Reprinted with permission from Keitner et al. 1987a. Copyright 1987 Grune & Stratton, Inc.

Table 4. Length of recovery period of FAD improvers versus nonimprovers

	Nonimprovers (months)	Improvers (months)
Problem solving	5.1 ± 3.0	5.4 ± 3.7
Communication	7.1 ± 4.3	4.5 ± 2.7
Roles	6.4 ± 3.8	4.3 ± 2.7
Affective responsiveness	6.2 ± 3.4	4.5 ± 3.2
Affective involvement*	7.0 ± 4.1	3.9 ± 1.9
Behavior control	5.0 ± 3.3	5.3 ± 3.4
General functioning*	8.1 ± 3.8	4.1 ± 2.4

Note. FAD = Family Assessment Device. Reprinted with permission from Keitner et al. 1987a. Copyright 1987 Grune & Stratton, Inc.
$^{*}P < .05$. $^{**}P < .01$.

Relapse and Family Functioning

A critical clinical question is whether the quality or type of family functioning is associated with recovery or relapse. That is, are patients in certain family environments more likely to have higher or lower rates of relapse? What can we tell families about the types of home environments most helpful or harmful to their ill members?

Vaughn and Leff (1976a) reported that depressed patients whose family members scored high on expressed emotions (EE—number of critical remarks made by key relatives in reference to the depressed patient) were three times as likely to relapse within 9 months as those patients whose relatives scored low on EE. Similar results were found in a replication study by Hooley et al. (1986) on 39 inpatients with major depression. Over a 9-month follow-up, 59% of patients with high-EE spouses relapsed, whereas no patient living with a low-EE spouse did so. Furthermore, depressed patients tended to relapse at lower rates of criticism than did schizophrenic patients. Interestingly, of the nine patients who did not relapse in high EE homes, seven were men.

EE ratings are derived from an interview with a relative by a researcher. [Editor's note: For a full discussion of the EE concept, see Chapter 3.] It is unclear to what extent behavior in such an artificial situation is representative of the relative's actual behavior with the patient. Hooley (1986) observed 39 clinically depressed patients and their spouses during a 10-minute face-to-face interaction. She found that, indeed, spouses rated as high EE were more negative and less positive both verbally and nonverbally than low-EE spouses. Patients with high-EE spouses, in turn, were less open, less expressive, and generally more passive than those with low-EE spouses.

Further reinforcing the importance of a nonstressful social environment was the finding by Brown and Prudo (1981) that provoking factors such as stressful life events are associated with an increased risk of relapse, especially in the presence of long-term vulnerability factors such as lack of supportive social networks. Similarly, Goering et al. (1983) also noted that lack of social support was a consistent predictor of relapse in depressed outpatients independent of symptom frequency.

In a mixed group of psychiatric patients (schizophrenia, affective disorders, substance abuse), Spiegel and Wissler (1986) found that several family environment variables were significant predictors of posthospital adjustment. Conflict in the family was associated with relapse, but an open, supportive discussion of feelings and problems in the family predicted reduced rehospitalization.

The above studies suggest that the family environment in which the depression evolves does have a significant relationship to the likelihood of recurrence of the depressive episode. A stressful, unsupportive, and, particularly, a critical social environment has been consistently found to be associated with a higher rate of relapse.

DISCUSSION

It is clear from our own research and from the literature reviewed that having a family member with major depression has a substantial impact on family functioning during the acute episode and at remission. Findings also suggest a significant relationship between family functioning and the duration of the depressive illness as well as the likelihood of relapse. There are a number of issues, however, that need to be delineated further before attempts can be made to use this information clinically. Particular issues that need further study relate to the causal relationship between family functioning and major depression, instrumentation used in assessing family functioning, the heterogeneity of depressive families, the congruence between perceptions of different family members, and sex differences in response to the depressive illness.

Causality

Currently, it is not clear whether problematic family relationships predispose to or permit the emergence of depressive illness or whether the depressive illness creates family difficulties in coping. There is evidence to support both points of view. An interactive mutually reinforcing negative pattern may be the best available explanation. There may be families in which the emergence of depressive illness in one (or more) member(s) creates undue strain because of the family's difficulty in coping with the illness. This perturbation in the family may further reinforce the prolongation of the depressive illness and/or its recurrence. This in turn creates further strains for the family.

Numerous studies suggest that personality variables and marital distress, not the depressive illness, are responsible for the family dysfunction. Rounsaville et al. (1980), for instance, suggested that marriages tend to be either good or disturbed over time and that if divorced and disputing depressed women remarried, they disputed with their new husbands as well. Because a number of depressed patients were able to sustain good marital environments, the personality of the depressed person was felt to be responsible for the marital strain, rather than the illness itself. Hops et al. (1987) felt that it was not the depressed mothers' family environments that were more aversive than those of nondepressed mothers, but rather that the depressed mothers themselves were more aversive to others. Again, the individual characteristics of the depressed person appear to create problems for other family members, rather than the family environment being destructive to the patient. Krantz and Moos (1987) also found that the spouse's adaptation in coping with the depressive illness was unrelated to changes in the depressive symptoms of the patient. Factors intrinsic to the situation and personalities of the members involved seemed to have a greater weight in determining response to the illness than the illness itself.

Menaghan (1985), looking at depressive affect and divorce rates, noted that persons who would subsequently divorce were not significantly more depressed before marital termination and that depressive affect was not a significant predictor of subsequent divorce. Emery et al. (1982) studied the school behavior of children of depressed and schizophrenic parents and noted that marital discord explained a greater proportion of the variance of children's school behavior than did the parental psychopathology. Interestingly, this was the case only for affectively disturbed patients, not for schizophrenic patients.

How, then, may the personality of the patient be interwoven with the depressive illness? Is it the depression that sets the stage for the development of problematic interpersonal styles, or is the personality dysfunction the primary cause? There is a rich but inconclusive literature on the interplay between personality and depression (Akiskal et al. 1983). Clearly, it is another variable that must be included in trying to understand the mutual influences between patients and family members.

Birtchnell and Kennard (1983) suggested that the mental health of women was more affected by bad marriages as opposed to the psychiatric illness causing the bad marriages. They felt that marital disturbances antedated the onset of depressive symptoms in the majority of cases. Similarly, Roy (1985, 1987) found that 70% of depressed patients reported a poor marriage before the onset of depression. He felt that, overall, a family history of depression and a poor marriage before the onset of depression were associated with the emergence of both endogenous and nonendogenous depression.

There is also evidence to suggest, however, that the depression itself creates a major burden and problem for the families of depressed patients. As noted previously, Coyne et al. (1987) and Fadden et al. (1987) have clearly documented the major impact that depressive illness has on the families of depressed patients.

On balance, the bulk of the evidence suggests that disturbed marriages and disturbed family environments serve a facilitating role for the emergence of depressive symptoms, particularly in those individuals vulnerable to developing a major depression. However, it is also clear that the depressive illness itself creates significant problems for those living with the depressed patient. There is no linear relationship between family dysfunction and depression, but rather a mutually interactive pattern is present. A depressive illness that, for various reasons, is difficult for a patient to bear creates significant problems for those living with that patient. If the family of this depressed patient does not have a clear understanding of and an appreciable way of dealing with the problems of the depression, then the depression itself can be significantly prolonged and worsened. Therapeutic interventions therefore need to address simultaneously the depressive illness and the family context in order to help all parties cope adequately, to minimize the risk of relapse, and to provide an atmosphere that can allow these approaches to work synergistically.

Measurement of Family Functioning

One of the difficulties in reviewing studies of depressed families is that a multitude of instruments are used to assess marital/family satisfaction, adjustment, or functioning. Some of these include the Social Adjustment Scale (Weissman 1975), KDS-15 (Frank and Kupfer 1974), Family Environment Scale (Moos and Moos 1981), Family Assessment Device (Epstein et al. 1983), Family Attitudes Questionnaire (Targum et al. 1981), Locke and Wallace Marital Adjustment Test (Locke and Wallace 1959), Camberwell Family Interview (Vaughn and Leff 1976b), Dyadic Adjustment Scale (Spanier 1976), Victoria Hospital Intimacy Interview (Waring et al. 1981), Marital Satisfaction Inventory (Snyder et al. 1981), and FACES-II (Olson et al. 1982).

It is beyond the scope of this chapter to review all of these instruments. Some are well validated and psychometrically tested. Others were not primarily designed to assess family parameters but some of their subscales have been used to describe family functioning. Still others were designed for a given study and do not have much psychometric support. The instruments range from simple questions concerning general satisfaction to schedules assessing multiple aspects of family life. The relative validity of the results reported is very difficult to assess accurately.

It is also unclear as to whether the same or similar family processes are being measured in these studies and to what extent the findings from the different studies can be merged. It is all the more striking then to note the remarkable uniformity of findings in different studies using widely disparate measures. Generally, almost all studies agree that significant disturbances are experienced by families through all stages of the depressive illness.

A second problem in the assessment of families is that very few studies have actually attempted to evaluate family functioning using objective measures. Most of the studies have used the perceptions of family members as a reflection of family functioning. Only a few have attempted to observe and rate these families using trained interviewers; fewer still have attempted to observe depressed patients in their home environments. At present, we can only say that family members perceive significant problems in their lives, but it is not clear to what extent this can be validated objectively and to what extent this distress, if objectively identifiable, is similar to or different from nonclinical families or from families in which other illnesses exist. In the final analysis perhaps it does not matter, because ultimately it is the distress felt by the patients and the families that requires clinical intervention.

Nevertheless, theoretically as well as practically, it would be helpful to have studies in which multiple validated instruments (both subjective and objective) of family functioning were used in the same population. We are in the process of completing one such study of depressed inpatients and their families during hospitalization, over the course of their illness, and at remission.

Congruence of Perceptions Between Different Family Members

In describing and measuring family functioning, the issue of weighing the different perceptions of various family members creates a difficult methodological problem. Should one describe each family member's perception and give each equal weight? Should this be the same whether there are two family members or six? Should the same weight be given to perceptions of children as to those of parents or grandparents? There are no easy answers to these questions.

For the sake of simplicity, our approach has been to use mean family scores in our preliminary analyses. At other times, discrepancies between different family members' perceptions can also be a useful indicator of particular types of problems. We have found, for instance, that a discrepancy between depressed patients' perceptions of their family environment and the perceptions of the rest of their family members is strongly associated with suicide attempts (Keitner et al. 1987b). In this study, depressed patients who had made active suicide attempts perceived their family functioning to be worse than did the rest of their family members, whereas depressed inpatients without suicide attempts actually saw their family functioning in a better light than did the rest of their family members. The depression itself then did not seem to be distorting the patients' perceptions of family functioning as might be expected based on cognitive theories.

Some studies have suggested that there is in fact good congruence between depressed persons' descriptions of their family functioning and those of other family members. Billings and Moos (1985b), for instance, noted that depressed patients' reports about family support and family arguments showed as much agreement with that of their nondepressed spouses as was observed for a matched community control group. Miller et al. (1986) also reported that excluding the patient's score from the mean family score did not produce significant changes in the severity or pattern of impairment found in families of patients with major depression, alcoholism, adjustment disorders, bipolar disorder, or schizophrenia. There was good agreement between these family members as well. Merikangas et al. (1985) also found that married couples (both depressed and nondepressed) had similar perceptions of marital functioning.

At this point, we do not know the best way to report family assessment measures. Further research is needed to determine not only if agreement between family members is common but, if there is disagreement, what this implies for the course of the illness, potential for relapse, or other clinically or theoretically important parameters.

Heterogeneity

Although DSM-III has helped to define depressive illness more clearly, major depression most likely consists of a number of different disorders. In addition, clinically one finds a variety of family and individual psychopathological problems in patients with major depression. At present, there is little research support for the hypothesis that a particular family constellation or interactional style invariably leads toward or is associated with major depression. Factors such as the premorbid functioning of the family, the developmental stage of the family, the health of other family members (particularly the absence or presence of psychiatric illness), the family's social and financial situation, and the availability of external supports all bear on the family's level of functioning and capacity to deal with crises including the current affective episode. There is also a marked heterogeneity found in patients themselves. Notable complicating factors are the finding of concurrent dysthymia and/or character disorders of various types in the depressed patient.

We have currently identified four broad groups of family types with respect to the depressive illness (Epstein et al. 1988). First, numerous patients with major depression have shown a remarkably rapid clearing of what appeared to be severe symptoms of depression once the family issues that were problematic were delineated and treated. Second, in some families there is minimal, if any, family pathology even during the acute phase of the illness of the identified patient. Third, there are groups of patients in whom a wide spectrum of family pathology is present, and patients and families all respond very well to the combination of pharmacologic and family therapy. In these patients, proper pharmacologic treatment improves the affective episode, and while this is occurring the patient and family work on their family problems during a course of family therapy. Fourth are groups of patients admitted with a wide range of very severe depressive symptomatology. These patients prove difficult to engage in any type of therapy, but once involved in family therapy plus antidepressant medication the depressive symptomatology disappears, only to reveal severe underlying character pathology and/or severe dysthymia, which in time proves impervious to further therapeutic efforts.

Other groupings may also have a significant impact on family response to the depressive illness. What is the importance, for instance, of having other coexisting Axis I diagnoses? Some depressive disorders coexist with various Axis II and Axis III disorders as well. The issue of assortative mating (Merikangas 1984) may also significantly influence the burden felt by other family members and the support available to the depressed person.

Many studies do not clearly identify the diagnosis of the depressed patients involved. Some studies focus on inpatient populations, others on outpatients, others on dysphoric populations only. Many studies combine depressed inpatients and outpatients and assume that the impact of the depression on the family in these cases is similar. We are not aware of any studies that take into consideration the coexistence of other concurrent illnesses, psychiatric or otherwise.

We are in the process of attempting to better understand this issue by following a sample of families of depressed inpatients, dividing them according to the parameters described above, and thereby trying to assess whether these factors play a significant role in the relationship between depression and family functioning.

Sex Differences

The suggestion of differences in the response of male and female patients to depressive illness is of considerable interest. It is well known that the prevalence of depression in women is two to three times as high as it is in men. Partly because of this, most studies looking at depression and family functioning have focused on women as patients. The few that have not have provided mixed results in terms of differential response patterns between men and women. However, certain patterns are evident that may deserve further study.

Hinchliffe et al. (1977) noted that males (patient and nonpatient) tended to show a greater shift in reducing tension over time as opposed to females (patient and nonpatient). Furthermore, women (as patient or spouse) attempted to control others more than men (Hooper et al. 1978). Crowther (1985) also noted that depressed men rated their marriages as significantly better adjusted than did depressed women. Hops et al. (1987) suggested that there may be some male/female differences in depressed families such that children in families with depressed mothers directed more aversive behavior at the mothers than at the fathers.

Our findings are suggestive of male/female differences, although possibly because of small numbers of males they have not reached statistical significance. We found in the families of depressed inpatients that when the patient was a male, family functioning was reported to be slightly better than when the patient was a female. Families of male and female patients improved to a similar degree, but at the remission of depression the families of male patients maintained their slight advantage over the families of female patients. There was no significant difference in time to recovery between male and female patients.

Bebbington (1987) has pointed out that marriages appear to be less protective for women than for men. Married men, for instance, have consistently lower rates of affective disorders than single men, whereas married women do not clearly have lower rates than their single counterparts.

As with other issues in this field, the question of sex differences remains unresolved, but certainly deserving of further research. Attempts should be made to study depressed families in which the patient is male to determine whether the same patterns as presently noted prevail and whether differential treatment interventions may be necessary depending on the sex of the identified patient.

CLINICAL IMPLICATIONS

There are some specific clinical implications from the studies reviewed. Given the substantial impact that marital distress and family turmoil have on the depressive illness and the major burden that is perceived by family members living with a depressed person, an approach to the treatment of depression that involves the whole family system seems self-evident. Unfortunately, empirical evidence to support this assumption is skimpy at best. This issue will be addressed in greater detail in subsequent chapters in this volume. There have been very few systematic studies to properly address this question. There is a real need for large-scale controlled studies to assess the effectiveness of family therapy in actually altering the course of the depressive illness. Until the results of such studies are available, we must continue to rely on clinical intuition and common sense.

The first step in the treatment of the depressed person is to become more fully aware of the social context in which the depression is unfolding. This means that, in addition to the history of the depressive symptoms, focus should be placed not only on obtaining the person's past social history, but also on assessing his or her current family situation. It is our practice to meet routinely with all family members living with the depressed person in order to develop a better understanding of the home environment that the depressed person comes from and returns to, and also to learn more about the expectations, worries, and complaints of individual family members.

An implicit agenda for these meetings is to ally ourselves not only with the patient but with other family members as well so that all family members feel supported and understood and are given an opportunity to have their particular concerns identified. The emphasis is on avoiding blame, concentrating instead on practical issues that need to be resolved. Establishing such a supportive alliance sets the stage for a collaborative effort that will not only help to reduce tensions that may be prevalent in the home, but will also improve compliance with present and future treatment recommendations.

Evidence from many studies suggesting continued family problems after the remission of the depression emphasizes the importance of continuing to be available to both patients and families even after remission of the depressive symptoms. This may take the form of follow-up visits or phone contacts spaced months apart, providing a sense of continuity and availability which may protect against the vicious cycles that may have been a part of the precipitation of previous episodes. At the very least, such contacts may have the effect of encouraging the patient and family members to identify early signs of relapse and to feel free in soliciting help at an early enough stage of the illness to facilitate rapid reinstitution of treatment.

We have found it very useful to have spouses and/or other family members continue to come with the patient for their regular follow-up visits. These visits may not involve family therapy, but often do involve sharing of information and providing support in coping with this debilitating illness. Even when patients are coming for "individual sessions," the presence of other family members provides an opportunity for them to learn how to handle the depressed patient, and for the depressed patient to feel more comfortable with the fact that their family members have a better understanding of their concerns and complaints. The boundaries between individual and family therapy are at times artificial and arbitrary. Although in certain circumstances confidentiality has to be maintained and specific issues may be unique to a given individual, in the majority of cases an undue concern about theoretical reasons for keeping individual and couples or family work separate is unwarranted and possibly detrimental.

At this point, we cannot predict the likely course and outcome of the depressive episode based on either the severity of the depression or the degree of turmoil or lack of turmoil in a particular family. Given this lack of ability to predict outcome, we feel that it is important to meet with the families of all patients and to provide the appropriate combination of treatment trials as the situation requires and as seems clinically necessary. Some patients who appear to have very disturbed family situations during the acute episode may in fact respond very quickly and well to the treatments provided, whereas other patients who seem to have well-settled and supportive families may in fact turn out to have more problems than is initially apparent.

There is no evidence to date to suggest that one form or type of family therapy is more or less effective in helping families with depressed members. The debate over specific or nonspecific therapeutic factors that is currently an issue for individual psychotherapy models also holds for family therapy. The issue of what type of family interventions may be helpful is reviewed in detail elsewhere in this book. We feel that at this point the specific techniques of carrying out the general principles we have outlined are less important than the fact of doing it.

The optimal treatment for a depressive episode includes the assessment of relevant biological, psychological, and social issues and the provision of appropriate intervention based on needs identified in such an assessment. Most patients will require some combination of the above approaches, including adequate pharmacotherapy, psychotherapy to address intrapsychic and interpersonal issues that cannot be resolved in therapy with the family, and family therapy to provide information about the illness and to modify those areas of family functioning that appear most problematic.

REFERENCES

Akiskal HS, Hirschfeld RMA, Yerevanian BI: The relationship of personality to affective disorders: a critical review. Arch Gen Psychiatry 40:801–810, 1983

American Psychiatric Association: Diagnostic and Statistical Manual of Mental Disorders, 3rd Edition. Washington, DC, American Psychiatric Association, 1980

Bebbington P: Marital status and depression: a study of English national admission statistics. Acta Psychiatr Scand 75:640–650, 1987

Biglan A, Hops H, Sherman L, et al: Problem-solving interactions of depressed women and their husbands. Behav Ther 16:431–451, 1985

Billings AG, Moos RH: Psychosocial processes in unipolar depression: comparing depressed patients with matched community controls. J Consult Clin Psychol 53:314–325, 1985a

Billings AG, Moos RH: Children of parents with unipolar depression: a controlled 1-year follow-up. J Abnorm Child Psychol 14:149–166, 1985b

Birtchnell J, Kennard J: Does marital maladjustment lead to mental illness? Soc Psychiatry 18:79–88, 1983

Bouras N, Vanger P, Bridges PK: Marital problems in chronically depressed and physically ill patients and their spouses. Compr Psychiatry 27:127–130, 1986

Brown GW, Prudo R: Psychiatric disorder in a rural and an urban population: 1. Aetiology of depression. 2. Sensitivity to loss. Psychol Med 11:581–599, 601–616, 1981

Corney RH: Marital problems and treatment outcome in depressed women: a clinical trial of social work intervention. Br J Psychiatry 151:652–659, 1987

Coyne JC, Kessler RC, Tal M, et al: Living with a depressed person. J Consult Clin Psychol 55:347–352, 1987

Crowther JH: The relationship between depression and marital maladjustment: a descriptive study. J Nerv Ment Dis 173:227–231, 1985

Dobson KS: Marital and social adjustment in depressed and remarried women. J Clin Psychol 43:261–265, 1987

Emery R, Weintraub S, Neale JM: Effects of marital discord on the school behavior of children of schizophrenic, affectively disordered, and normal parents. J Abnorm Child Psychol 10:215–228, 1982

Epstein NB, Bishop DS, Levin S: The McMaster model of family functioning. Journal of Marriage and Family Counseling 4:19–31, 1978

Epstein NB, Baldwin LM, Bishop DS: The McMaster family assessment device. Journal of Marital and Family Therapy 9:171–180, 1983

Epstein NB, Keitner GI, Bishop DS, et al: Combined use of pharmacological and family therapy, in Affective Disorders and the Family Assessment and Treatment. Edited by Clarkin JF, Haas G, Glick I. New York, Guilford Press, 1988

Fadden G, Bebbington P, Kuipers L: Caring and its burdens: a study of the spouses of depressed patients. Br J Psychiatry 151:660–667, 1987

Frank E, Kupfer DJ: The KDS-15: a marital questionnaire. Western Psychiatric Institute. Pittsburgh, University of Pittsburgh, 1974

Goering P, Wasylenki D, Lancee W, et al: Social support and post hospital outcome for depressed women. Can J Psychiatry 28:612–618, 1983

Hinchliffe M, Hooper D, Roberts FJ, et al: A study of the interaction between depressed patients and their spouses. Br J Psychiatry 126:164–172, 1975

Hinchliffe M, Vaughan PW, Hooper D, et al: The melancholy marriage: an inquiry into the interaction of depression, II: Expressiveness. Br J Med Psychol 50:125–142, 1977

Hooley JM: Expressed emotion and depression: interactions between patients and high- versus low-expressed-emotion spouses. J Abnorm Psychol 95:237–246, 1986

Hooley JM, Orley J, Teasdale JD: Levels of expressed emotion and relapse in depressed patients. Br J Psychiatry 148:642–647, 1986

Hooper D, Vaughan PW, Hinchliffe MK, et al: The melancholy marriage: an inquiry into the interaction of depression. V. Power. Br J Med Psychol 51:387–398, 1978

Hops H, Biglan A, Sherman L, et al: Home observations of family interactions of depressed women. J Consult Clin Psychol 55:341–346, 1987

Keitner GI, Baldwin LM, Epstein NB, et al: Family functioning in patients with affective disorders: a review. International Journal of Family Psychiatry 6:405–437, 1985

Keitner GI, Miller IW, Epstein NB, et al: The functioning of families in patients with major depression. International Journal of Family Psychiatry 7:11–16, 1986

Keitner GI, Miller IW, Epstein NB, et al: Family functioning and the course of major depression. Compr Psychiatry 28:54–64, 1987a

Keitner GI, Miller IW, Fruzzetti AE, et al: Family functioning and suicidal behavior in psychiatric inpatients with major depression. Psychiatry 50:242–255, 1987b

Krantz SE, Moos RH: Functioning and life context among spouses of remitted and nonremitted depressed patients. J Consult Clin Psychol 55:353–360, 1987

Locke HJ, Wallace KM: Short marital adjustment and prediction tests: their reliability and validity. Marriage and Family Living 21:251–255, 1959

Menaghan EG: Depressive affect and subsequent divorce. Journal of Family Issues 6:295–306, 1985

Merikangas KR: Divorce and assortative mating among depressed patients. Am J Psychiatry 141:74–76, 1984

Merikangas KR, Prusoff BA, Kupfer DJ, et al: Marital adjustment in major depression. J Affective Disord 9:5–11, 1985

Miller IW, Bishop DS, Epstein NB, et al: The McMaster family assessment device: reliability and validity. Journal of Marital and Family Therapy 4:345–356, 1985

Miller IW, Kabacoff RI, Keitner GI, et al: Family functioning in the families of psychiatric patients. Compr Psychiatry 27:302–312, 1986

Moos RJ, Moos BS: Family Environment Scale Manual. Palo Alto, CA, Consulting Psychologists Press, 1981

Nock SL, Rossi PH: Household types and social standings. Social Forces 57:1325–1345, 1979

Olson DH, Portner J, Bell R: FACES-II: family adaptability and cohesion evaluation scales. St. Paul, MN, Family Social Science, University of Minnesota, 1982

Rounsaville BJ, Weissman MM, Prusoff BA, et al: Marital disputes and treatment outcome in depressed women. Compr Psychiatry 20:483–490, 1979

Rounsaville BJ, Prusoff BA, Weissman MM: The course of marital disputes in depressed women: a 48-month follow-up study. Compr Psychiatry 21:111–118, 1980

Roy A: Depression and marriage. Psychiatr J Univ Ottawa 10:101–103, 1985

Roy A: Five risk factors for depression. Br J Psychiatry 150:536–541, 1987

Snyder DK, Wills RM, Keiser TW: Empirical validation of the Marital Satisfaction Inventory: an actuarial approach. J Consult Clin Psychol 49:262–268, 1981

Spanier GB: Measuring dyadic adjustment: new scales for assessing the quality of marriage and other dyads. Journal of Marital and Family Therapy 38:15–28, 1976

Spiegel D, Wissler T: Family environment as a predictor of psychiatric hospitalization. Am J Psychiatry 143:56–60, 1986

Targum SD, Dibble ED, Davenport YB, et al: The Family Attitudes Questionnaire: patients' and spouses' views of bipolar illness. Arch Gen Psychiatry 38:562–568, 1981

Vaughn CE, Leff JP: The influence of family and social factors on the course of psychiatric illness. Br J Psychiatry 129:125–137, 1976a

Vaughn CE, Leff JP: The measurement of expressed emotion in the families of psychiatric patients. Br J Soc Clin Psychol 15:157–165, 1976b

Waring EM, Patton D: Marital intimacy and depression. Br J Psychiatry 145:641–644, 1984

Waring EM, McElrath D, Mitchell P, et al: Intimacy and emotional illness in the general population. Can J Psychiatry 26:167–172, 1981

Weissman MM: The assessment of social adjustment: a review of techniques. Arch Gen Psychiatry 32:357–365, 1975

Weissman M, Paykel E: The Depressed Woman: A Study of Her Relationships. Chicago, IL, University of Chicago Press, 1974

Chapter 2

Interpersonal Processes in Depression

James C. Coyne, Ph.D.

Chapter 2

Interpersonal Processes in Depression

There is a long-standing bias toward viewing depressed persons and their complaints in isolation from their interpersonal context. Currently, this is evident in cognitive theories of depression that narrowly focus on the purportedly biased and distorted thinking of depressed persons and in biological theories of depression that do not allow for interpersonal factors possibly influencing biological variables or the course of a depressive episode.

In recent decades, there have indeed been tremendous increases in our understanding of the biology of depression, and the efficacy of antidepressant medication has been well established. Yet, these advances in no way contradict the need to understand better the interpersonal circumstances of depressed persons. Even when there is strong evidence that there is a biological component to a depressive episode, interpersonal factors are likely to have served as a precipitant, and they may be an important determinant of the response to treatment and how the episode is resolved, what the cost is to the family as well as the patient, what residual problems remain, and what the likelihood of relapse is. When an adequately comprehensive model of depression is ultimately developed, interpersonal processes will have a key role along with biological factors.

Even though Harry Stack Sullivan did so much to promote an interpersonal perspective in American psychiatry, he largely ignored the affective disorders (Coyne et al. 1987a). It is only recently that the study of interpersonal processes in depression has begun to achieve momentum. Our understanding of these processes remains limited and, for the most part, consists of provocative findings that particular phenomena co-occur, rather than a sense of precisely how they are linked. Thus, although there is evidence that spousal criticism at the time of hospitalization predicts subsequent relapse (Hooley et al. 1986; Vaughn and Leff 1976), we can only speculate about the mechanism that is involved. The explanation of some findings remains even more elusive, such as that being in an enduring close relationship is associated with poorer outcomes in treatment with antidepressant medication (Keller et al. 1984). To the extent to which such findings can be replicated, there is the suggestion of complex links between interpersonal and biological processes that deserve considerably more attention than they have received.

Some well-established myths about the nature of depression pose barriers to a better understanding of interpersonal processes in the disorder. First and most basically, there is the tendency to interpret distinctions between endogenous and nonendogenous depressions as if they represented a rigid division between those depressions for which we can afford to ignore the role of interpersonal factors and those depressions for which there is some relevance of interpersonal factors. To the contrary, there is evidence that endogenously depressed patients tend to have preexisting problems in their close relationships (Birchnell and Kennard 1983), and the overall association among depressed patients between endogenous features and the presence or absence of recent life events is weak at best (Dolan et al. 1985). Reactivity to changes in the environment *during* a depressive episode, rather than the absence of precipitating stress, has been found to predict response to biologically oriented treatment (Fowles and Gershon 1979) and has now replaced the lack of antecedent stress as a criterion for endogenicity.

Second, with the influence of cognitive theories of depression (i.e., Beck 1976), there is the tendency to dismiss the complaints of depressed persons about their close relationships and how they are treated by others as reflecting their distorted perceptions. As we will see, evidence from other sources provides substantiation for depressed persons' complaints about conflict, rejection, and a lack of support in their lives. Depressed persons are likely to be engaged in interpersonal struggles, particularly in their close relationships, that serve to perpetuate their distress, and a failure to resolve these struggles is an important source of vulnerability to relapse.

At the outset, it should be reiterated that the findings that will be cited are suggestive rather than indicative of the complex processes by which depressed persons and those around them are influencing each other. We are also handicapped by the lack of a theoretical model that is adequate to the task of integrating these diverse findings. Further, we know considerably more about the situations of depressed women than we know about those of depressed men. However, even if much of the evidence is circumstantial, it is consistent in suggesting that there are rich and reciprocal links between depressed persons and their interpersonal environments. This overview will start with interpersonal factors in vulnerability to depression and the onset of an episode and will proceed to a consideration of what is known about interpersonal processes during an acute episode and then to possible influences on the resolution of an episode, residual difficulties, and relapse.

LIFE EVENTS, INTIMACY, AND DEPRESSION

Exposure to severe life events and, to a lesser degree, chronic difficulties plays an important role in the onset of depression, even though these factors in themselves are insufficient to explain fully its occurrence. Paykel (1979) has calculated that, taking into account the occurrence of any of the major life events that he examined, the risk of depression is increased by a factor of 5.6 in the 6 months after the event. An event involving an exit from a significant role increases the risk of depression by a factor of 6.5.

Brown and Harris (1978) found that the relationship between severe life events and depression held across inpatient, outpatient, general practitioner, and community samples. For instance, in a sample of community-residing women, 53% of the women with newly diagnosed depression had a severe life event of causal importance in the previous 9 months versus 19% of the women who were not depressed. Only events that had long-term threatening implications for a woman's well-being brought about depression, and thus, studies that do not distinguish between these and other types of life events may obtain a lower estimate of their causal significance. Brown and Harris (1978) also found that

> The distinctive feature of the great majority of the provoking events is the experience of loss or disappointment, if this is defined broadly to include threat of or actual separation from a key figure, an unpleasant revelation about someone else, a life-threatening illness to a close relative, a major material loss or general disappointment or threat of them, and miscellaneous crises such as being made redundant after a long period of steady employment. (pp. 274–275)

Whether stressful life events are implicated in a depressive episode is relatively independent of whether there are identifiable biological features. It appears, for example, that the presence of antecedent life events is not related to whether nonsuppression of cortisol secretion occurs in response to dexamethasone (Dolan et al. 1985). A history of previous episodes predicts depression in the apparent absence of severe life events, but the reasons for this have not been established.

Age better explains the relationship between number of previous episodes and the absence of antecedent life events than the number of episodes explains the relationship between age and the absence of events (Brown and Harris 1978). Beyond that, it is unclear whether depression in the apparent absence of life events is indicative of processes that have become independent of interpersonal circumstances or indicative of an increased susceptibility to circumstances that would not be considered a severe threat for someone who is younger or without such a history of previous depressive episodes.

Many life events associated with depression represent disturbances in close relationships, and the single most frequent event reported by depressed women is an increase in arguments with their spouses (Paykel et al. 1969). It has been suggested that chronic disturbance in enduring close relationships may be a more common cause of depression than actual disruption of these relationships (Coyne and DeLongis 1986). On the other hand, a positive, confiding relationship with the spouse represents an important source of resistance to depression, although this may be more true for women than for men (Coyne and DeLongis 1989), and controversy remains as to whether the contribution of an intimate relationship is primarily direct or as a buffer against the effects of life events (Brown and Harris 1978; Cleary and Kessler 1982; Everitt and Smith 1979).

Women who have an intimate relationship with their spouse are only one-third as likely to become depressed in the face of life events as those who do not, and having a good intimate relationship neutralizes the effects of other risk factors such as having three young children at home, being unemployed, and having lost one's mother in childhood (Brown and Harris 1978). Although intimacy may be associated with resistance to depression, there are gaps in our knowledge as to the determinants of whether a woman has an intimate relationship and precisely how such intimacy protects against depression.

Adjustment problems and personal vulnerabilities of the spouses of depressed persons may limit them as sources of intimacy. Brown et al. (1986) found that over two-thirds of the women in their sample who lacked a quality relationship with their spouses were married to men whom raters considered "grossly undependable" as mates, parents, and providers. Depressed persons, particularly women, have a tendency to be married to spouses with personal and family histories of psychiatric disturbance, and depressed women tend to be married to men with personality disorders (Negri et al. 1979; Merikangas and Spiker 1982). Marriage tends to have occurred before the first treated episode of depression, and the choice of mate may have limited the possibilities for achievement of a positive, intimate relationship. However, almost all of the studies of assortative mating have been conducted with hospitalized or incarcerated populations, and so replication with outpatient depressed samples is sorely needed.

Studies by Quinton et al. (1984) and Parker and Hadzi-Pavlovic (1984) provide some suggestions as to how early experience might influence mate selection and subsequent proneness to depression. These studies focused on psychiatric disturbance (mainly depression) and parenting among women who had especially adverse childhood experiences, such as being reared in an institution after death of the mother. On the whole, these women were quite prone to psychiatric disturbance and marital and parenting difficulties, but the minority of women who were largely free of disturbance or social difficulties had good, supportive relationships with their spouses. Whether they had such positive relationships with their spouses was tied in part to whether their spouses were currently having alcohol or drug problems or difficulties with the law. Furthermore, spouses' reports of their own problems in adolescence—generally *before* they met their future wives—predicted whether their wives had problems *at present*. Thus, the effects of early childhood experience on depression may be largely indirect and through the selection of the spouse and the quality of the marital relationship that is achieved. Taken together, these studies suggest that depression-prone women may be more likely to be married to men with difficulties of their own and who may be less able to provide the secure, intimate relationship that would reduce the women's risk of depression. How such men and women select each other and how each other's vulnerabilities get expressed and shape their relationship deserve further study.

The processes by which having an intimate relationship reduces the risk of depression are not clear, but it is unlikely to be via a single mechanism. A high degree of intimacy may be only one aspect of a relationship in which there is also less conflict, fewer serious disappointments, and a diminished threat of separation or divorce. Also, an intimate relationship may provide a secure source of meaning and self-esteem in the face of threatening events arising outside the marital relationship, and it may serve to preserve the sense of confidence that one's circumstances are predictable and that things will work out as well as can reasonably be expected. The opportunities for self-disclosure, validation, and corrective emotional experiences provided by an intimate relationship may also serve to counter negative experiences that might otherwise result in depression. Finally, a spouse with whom there is a positive, intimate relationship may be more actively and collaboratively involved in the process of coping with a stressful life event in a way that reduces the burden or threat to the person at risk.

In summary, whether or not they possess endogenous features, depressive episodes tend to be antedated by stressful events having long-term threat to a person's well-being. Close relationships are both a frequent source of such events and a potentially powerful source of resistance to depression. The likelihood of a marital relationship being either a source of precipitating events or of resistance to depression may depend in part on mate selection and characteristics that both spouses bring to the relationship. Although the achievement of a quality, intimate relationship with the spouse is important, particularly for women otherwise at risk for depression, the processes linking intimacy to reduced risk are unclear at this time.

INTERPERSONAL PROCESSES DURING A DEPRESSIVE EPISODE

Depressed persons tend to have difficulties with others. As was just noted, some of these difficulties precede and contribute to the onset of an episode. Some reflect an aversiveness to depressed persons that may emerge in even a brief encounter with a stranger, whereas other difficulties are confined to close relationships. The spouses and children of depressed persons are themselves at considerable risk for psychological distress. Yet, it is clear that these findings reflect complex interpersonal processes that cannot be reduced to the unilateral influence of depressed persons on those around them or vice versa.

Toward a Model

Coyne (1976a) provided a preliminary explanation of how the behavior of depressed persons and those around them might come to fit into an emergent interpersonal system. The distressed behavior of depressed persons may be seen as reflecting involvement in a situation in which the usual sources of security, meaning, and validation have been disrupted or have otherwise proven to be insufficient. The obvious distress of depressed persons has the effect of engaging others, making them feel responsible, and shifting the interactional burden onto them. This distress proves aversive to others and is capable of inducing negative moods in them. Yet, at the same time, it is also guilt inducing and inhibiting. People around depressed persons may attempt to control or reduce the aversiveness of depressed persons by seemingly providing what is being asked, even while communicating impatience, hostility, and rejection. The subtle and overt hostility and rejection that depressed persons receive validates their sense of insecurity and elicits further expression of distress, strengthening the pattern. Thus, others may become involved with depressed persons in ways that unwittingly perpetuate or aggravate their problems.

More recent statements of this formulation have acknowledged the salience of overt anger and negative outbursts in the interactions of depressed persons and how these features might be related to inhibited communication at other times and the resulting accumulation of unresolved issues (Kahn et al. 1985). Related to this, the Oregon Research Institute group has used Patterson and Reid's (1970) coercion theory in conceptualizing depressive behavior as a form of aversive control and emphasizes how displays of depressive behavior may inhibit hostile behavior and elicit compliance from others in the short run, even if it does not reduce their subsequent hostility (Biglan et al. 1988). Finally, it has also been suggested how the patterning of behavior in which depressed persons and intimates become involved can be expected to interfere with their ability to have positive interactions, maintain a household, solve their problems, and renegotiate their relationship (Coyne 1988). Yet, even with such elaborations and qualifications, this conceptualization of depression provides an incomplete picture of interpersonal processes in depression, although it has served to kindle interest in these processes.

Depression in Fleeting Contacts Between Strangers

Findings that depressed persons and intimates have problems are by themselves ambiguous in that these difficulties might be interpreted as effects of mate selection or of any preexisting conflict or negative attitudes that the depressed persons and their spouses have toward each other. For this reason, laboratory studies in which depressed persons interact with others who have not had any previous negative experiences with them may prove important in elucidating some of the processes occurring in the close relationships of depressed persons. In the first of numerous studies of encounters between depressed persons and strangers, Coyne (1976b) found that naive subjects who engaged in a 20-minute telephone conversation with depressed outpatients showed negative changes in mood and negatively evaluated and rejected the outpatients. Subsequent studies have almost all found that depressed persons are negatively received, and effects on the mood of others are often found. (See Gurtman 1986 and Coyne et al. 1987a for reviews.) The effects of depressed persons on others may be both subtle and immediate. Changes in nonverbal behavior are evident 3 minutes into naive persons' interactions with mildly depressed persons (Gotlib and Robinson 1982). In interviews with physicians, it has been found that the severity of a patient's depression is more readily reflected in the physician's nonverbal behavior than in the patient's (Frey et al. 1980). Simply being told that someone is depressed leads to others sitting further away before an interaction starts (Yarkin et al. 1981).

Precisely what depressed persons do that leads them to evoke such responses, to be liked less, and to be negatively evaluated remains elusive. Various studies have found them to speak in a monotonous tone, avoid eye contact, and time their self-disclosures inappropriately, but such differences are less reliably found than are others' reports of a negative impact of the depressed persons on them (Coyne et al. 1987a). Further, some of depressed persons' supposed deficits in interpersonal skills may reflect how others are treating them. Although depressed persons make fewer positive responses to others in a group situation, they also receive fewer positive responses (Libet and Lewinsohn 1973). After a brief interaction with mildly depressed persons, others report being less honest with them (Strack and Coyne 1983). However, when given frank feedback, depressed inpatients are just as likely to adjust their interpersonal behavior as other persons are (Herbert et al. 1988).

Two studies of the game behavior of mildly depressed persons contradict the stereotype that they are passive and lack outwardly directed hostility. Whether such findings replicate with more severely depressed persons remains to be seen. Hokanson et al. (1980) found that when placed in a high-power role, depressed persons tended to be exploitive and noncooperative, and they communicated more self-devaluation and helplessness. In response to this, their partners showed more noncooperativeness, extrapunitiveness, and expressions of helplessness. When placed in a low-power role by the experimenter, depressed persons tended to blame their partners, and this elicited more friendliness and ingratiating behavior from their partners. When confederates adopted a critical-competitive role, they elicited more extrapunitiveness from depressed than from nondepressed subjects, and when confederates acted helpless and dependent, they elicited more negative self-statements from depressed than from nondepressed subjects (Blumberg and Hokanson 1983). Across confederate roles, depressed persons communicated high levels of self-devaluation, sadness, helplessness, and general negative content.

Of course, enduring close relationships place more complex demands on depressed persons than brief laboratory interactions with strangers, and we should be cautious about uncritical generalizations from these studies to what must occur in the marriages and families of depressed persons. The same caution should be applied in generalizing findings from "mildly depressed" subjects to those meeting diagnostic criteria for major depression. One might even hypothesize that close relationships should be more tolerant and forgiving of depressed persons' difficulties than are strangers, yet, as we will see, what is found in these relationships is negativity and conflict. The studies of depressed persons' interactions with strangers are helpful in suggesting that some of these problems may represent the evolving patterning of depression and the response of others, rather than simply the continuance of preexisting problems.

Depression and the Marital Relationship

In an early study, Weissman and Paykel (1974) found that although the difficulties of depressed women extended into all of their social roles, including worker and member of the community, they faced their greatest problems as wives and mothers. Structured interviews with these women indicated that their marriages were characterized by friction, hostility, poor communication, dependency, and diminished sexual satisfaction.

Subsequent studies have found that the marriages of depressed persons are beset by problems, including general dissatisfaction and overt conflict. The laboratory interactions of depressed persons and their spouses are uncomfortable, tense, and hostile. These interactions are characterized by disruptions and negative outbursts, discrepancies between verbal content and tone of both spouses, avoidance and withdrawal, and little constructive problem solving (Arkowitz et al. 1982; Hinchliffe et al. 1978; Kahn et al. 1985; Hautzinger et al. 1982; McLean et al. 1973). Studies have found important similarities between depressed persons and their spouses in their overt hostility and lack of constructive problem solving (Kahn et al. 1985), but also differences in that depressed persons speak more negatively about themselves, whereas their spouses speak negatively about their depressed partners and disclose little about themselves (Hautzinger et al. 1982). Sequential analyses have shown that depressed women's displays of distress tend to inhibit their husbands' aggressiveness temporarily, but aggressiveness by husbands also inhibits their wives' subsequent depressive behavior (Biglan et al. 1985). The interactions between depressed persons and spouses are considerably more negative than those between depressed persons and strangers (Hinchliffe et al. 1978), and differences in the marital interactions of couples with and without a depressed partner persist when marital dissatisfaction is controlled (Hautzinger et al. 1982). Other studies suggest that depressed women concede more in disagreements with their husbands (Merikangas et al. 1979), and that they are more likely than nondepressed women to be dominated by their husbands in decision making (Hoover and Fitzgerald 1981).

The self-complaints of depressed persons and their feelings of insecurity may be more congruent with the nature of their relationships with their spouses than has generally been supposed. Thus, Leff and Vaughn (1985) found that the majority of depressed patients, particularly women, were fearful of loss and rejection and desirous of continual comfort and support. Yet, contextualizing this observation, Leff and Vaughn (1985) showed how depression may be maintained in such fears and perceptions—namely—"few depressed patients described as chronically insecure or lacking in self-confidence were living with supportive or sympathetic spouses . . . when this was the case, the patients were well at follow-up" (p. 95).

Leff and Vaughn (1985) found that the majority of the spouses of depressed persons were critical of them. Although some of this criticism centered on their depressed partners' current symptomatic behavior, a considerable proportion of it was aimed at traits and behavior evident before the onset of the patients' depression. Such a hostile, critical environment can be the origin of depressed persons' self-complaints and hopelessness, a means of validating and expanding on existing self-criticism, and a buffer against change. Consistent with this latter possibility, experimental studies suggest that intimates who agree with a person's negative self-view can effectively insulate that person from positive experiences that might otherwise challenge this view of themselves (Swann and Predmore 1985).

Overall, examination of the marital relationships of depressed persons suggests that their distress, problems such as dependency and inhibition, and difficulties dealing with hostility do not occur in a vacuum, and the fit of these difficulties with the patterning of their close relationships warrants more attention. There is considerable evidence that their problems reflect their involvement in a marital situation that is distressing and insecure and not conducive to renegotiating expectations, to overt disagreement, or to the direct expression of negative affect. Further, rather than simply being passive and withdrawn, depressed persons are often caught up in miscarried efforts to resolve their difficulties with intimates in which they are unsuccessfully confrontational as well. As Kahn et al. (1985) suggested, depressed persons and their spouses may be involved in a cycle in which their unsuccessful efforts to resolve differences lead to withdrawal and avoidance and to negative affect, mistrust, and misgivings about each other. The accumulated effect of such interactions is to overwhelm the couple when they again attempt to settle specific differences, increasing their hopelessness about the possibility of improving their relationship.

Apparently, such relationships are a source of distress for spouses as well. In our own work, we found that 40% of the spouses of depressed persons had serious enough distress to meet a standardized criteria for referral for psychiatric intervention (Coyne et al. 1987b). When patients had recovered, only 17% of the spouses met this criteria. Further analyses of these data revealed that the degree of burden experienced by persons living with a patient in an acute depressive episode versus those living with one who had recovered accounted entirely for their differences in distress levels. In descending magnitude, the specific burdens rated as being the most serious problems were the patient's lack of energy, the emotional strain on the respondent, the possibility that the patient would become depressed again, the patient's sense of worthlessness, and the patient's lack of interest in doing things.

Rush et al. (1980) suggested that "the spouse of the depressed person cannot be considered neutral. He or she becomes frustrated, confused, overly solicitous, or angry, or withdrawn emotionally" (p. 105). The picture emerging from recent research is even more complex. Spouses may have precipitated many of the difficulties of depressed persons, and they may be actively involved in their perpetuation. It is clear that conceptualization of these difficulties simply in terms of the role impairments or social skill deficits of depressed persons is much too narrow. At the same time, we should avoid swinging to the other extreme of seeing depression as simply a matter of the depressed person's victimization by a critical and unsupportive spouse. There is a definite burden associated with living with a depressed person. We need to develop an appreciation of how difficult the close relationships of depressed persons are for all involved, how they came to be this way, and how they can be effectively modified.

Children of Depressed Patients

The children of a depressed parent are at risk for a full range of psychological problems, academic difficulties, and even physical health problems. [Editor's note: For a more complete discussion of this area, see Chapters 4 and 5.] As many as 40–50% of the children of a depressed parent have a diagnosable psychiatric disturbance (Cytryn et al. 1982; Decina et al. 1983; for a review see Coyne et al. 1987a). Problems are apparent shortly after birth (Sameroff et al. 1982) and throughout infancy and early childhood (Sameroff et al. 1985; Seifer et al. 1981), primary school years (Cohler et al. 1977; Fisher et al.

1980; Neale and Weintraub 1975; Weintraub et al. 1978), and adolescence (Hirsch et al. 1985). Some studies have suggested that the risk for disturbance among the children of depressed parents is as great as or greater than the risk of disturbance among the offspring of schizophrenic parents (Weintraub et al. 1978; Sameroff et al. 1985), and the risk seems greater with "neurotically depressed" rather than more severely depressed parents (Fisher et al. 1980), and with unipolar rather than bipolar parents (Sameroff et al. 1985).

The parenting behavior of depressed parents has frequently been implicated in their children's problems. During a depressive episode, depressed mothers report being less involved with their children, and they are more resentful of them than are nondepressed mothers (Weissman and Paykel 1974). They also report being less affectionate and more emotionally distant, irritable, and preoccupied, and they experience guilt and difficulty communicating with their children. They direct even more hostility toward their children than toward their spouses. Other sources describe depressed parents both as being overprotective and putting their children into the role of parents (Drake and Price 1975) and as having an impoverished ability to provide emotionally for their children (Zahn-Waxler et al. 1984).

Yet, it would be a mistake to conclude prematurely that the serious problems of the children of depressed persons are simply a direct result of the depressed parent's dysfunction. Problems in the families of depressed persons are more pervasive. The Brown University Family Research Group (Miller et al. 1986) found that families of patients with major depression consistently reported poorer levels of family functioning than families of patients with diagnoses of bipolar disorder, manic; schizophrenia; adjustment disorder; and alcohol dependence. This held true even when the reports of the patients were excluded from analyses. The families of patients with major depressive disorder reported worse fuctioning for all dimensions of the Family Assessment Device (Epstein et al. 1983): problem solving, communication, roles, affective responsiveness, affective involvement, behavior control, and general functioning.

Further, the problems of the children may depend on the adjustment of the depressed person's spouse and whether there are marital problems or disruption. Thus, the risk of child disturbance increases when both parents are disturbed (Kuyler et al. 1980; Weissman et al. 1984). The nondepressed parent being available and supportive may substantially reduce the risk to these children (Fisher et al., in press). Emery et al. (1982) concluded that in the absence of marital difficulties the risk of problematic school behavior among the offspring of an affectively disturbed parent was no greater than among the offspring of normal control parents. Other studies have found that families in which there has been a divorce account for a considerable proportion of the psychological disturbance of children of depressed parents (Conners et al. 1979; Kuyler et al. 1980).

There has been little attention to the reciprocal effects of children's behavior on their depressed parents. However, the Oregon Research Institute group has found that children of depressed women exhibit more irritation in the presence of their mothers than do the children of nondepressed mothers (Biglan et al. 1988; Friedman 1984). Displays of distress by depressed mothers reduced their children's irritated and aggressive behavior, but it also reduced their caring behavior.

Parental depression is thus associated with major threats to the well-being of children. However, when we begin to examine the broader family context of depression, questions arise as to whether the depressed parent's behavior is the only or the most critical influence on the children. As at other points in this review, we are left with a clear association between depression and the problems of others, but an ambiguous picture as to the interpersonal processes determining this association. As research accumulates, we should be prepared to find complex, reciprocal processes, involving not only the influence of the depressed parents on their children, but also of the other parent on the relationship between the depressed parent and the children. Further research has much to gain from better assessment of family functioning and from greater attention to support and stress coming from outside the mother-child dyad and outside the immediate family. Finally, acting out and dysfunctional children can be a significant source of stress and disappointment for an already-depressed parent, and the effect of the children's problems on the functioning of the depressed parent and the family is also worth considering.

INTERPERSONAL PROCESSES AND THE COURSE OF DEPRESSION

For many depressed persons, recovery may require renegotiation or even termination of their troubled relationship. [Editor's note: For additional discussion of this area, see Chapter 1.] There have been repeated serendipitous findings that depressed persons who have recently ended an intimate relationship fare better than those whose relationships endure. This has been found with patients receiving antidepressant medication (Keller et al. 1984) or psychotherapy for depression (Parker et al. 1985) and among persons who have been identified as depressed cases among general practice patients (Parker et al. 1986) or drawn from a community sample (Parker and Blignault 1985). In the absence of further data, we can speculate that it may be easier to recover from the ending of a relationship than for some depressed persons to renegotiate their chronically distressing relationships.

Stronger associations are found between marital problems and poor outcomes. Courney (1984) found that depressed women with marital problems were less likely to improve in individual psychotherapy than those without problems. Although cognitive therapy has proven to be effective with depressed outpatients, Jacobson et al. (1987) found that depressed persons with marital problems benefited little from it.

The Yale group (Rounsaville et al. 1979) has found that the marital problems faced by many depressed persons are also a negative prognostic indicator in treatment with antidepressant medication. Those patients whose marriages improve show satisfactory responses to medication, but the evidence is that medication had little direct effect on the quality of depressed persons' involvement in their marriages (Weissman et al. 1981). Further, 4-year follow-up assessment of depressed persons with marital problems who have been treated with antidepressants suggests that they tend to continue to be vulnerable to depression and to have marital problems (Rounsaville et al. 1980). Families' initial reports of their functioning during an acute episode are apparently not good predictors of the length of patients' depression, but depressed patients whose families subsequently showed some improvement in general functioning have shorter depressive episodes than those who did not (Keitner et al. 1987). Two studies have shown that the number of critical comments made by a spouse about a depressed patient in an interview during the patient's hospitalization are strongly predictive of subsequent relapse (Hooley et al. 1986). Spousal criticism is a better predictor of relapse than is the patient's initial severity of symptoms, and it continues to work as a predictor after controlling for severity of symptoms.

Findings from numerous studies suggest that on patients' recovery, there is improvement in marital and family functioning, but that problems persist. Weissman and Paykel (1974) found that although there was improvement in most areas of marital functioning with symptomatic recovery, depressed women tended to have more problems than normal controls in the areas of interpersonal friction and inhibited communication with their spouses. It appears that communication in couples with a depressed man improves more with the patients' recovery than in couples with a depressed woman (Hinchliffe et al. 1978). Families of recovered depressed patients still report worse functioning than the families of nonpatients in terms of problem-solving skills, communication, and overall functioning (Keitner et al. 1987). At a 1-year follow-up, Billings and Moos (1985) found that little change had occurred in the children of depressed patients. Although children of patients who demonstrated symptomatic remission had fewer reported problems than did children of nonremitted patients, these children were still more symptomatic than were the children of controls.

Thus, studies indicate potentially rich associations between interpersonal processes and the course and outcome of depression. The various data reviewed suggest that disharmony in close relationships may have an impact on the course of depression, and that continued problems may impede the recovery process, limit the response to treatment, and even be associated with higher rates of relapses. Findings were noted that indicated that depressed persons were at continued risk for interpersonal problems beyond the acute episode, that such problems predict persistence or recurrence of depression, and that the difficulties of their children also persist beyond the acute episode. These findings add to the weight of evidence challenging traditional notions that depression is a matter of singular occurrence or discrete episodes that are resolved with little residual difficulties (Weissman et al. 1976). Depression may have a highly variable course, but it is more frequently a refractory problem than has been assumed. The intractability of depressed persons' interpersonal difficulties deserves greater attention as a factor in chronic and recurrent depression.

SUMMARY AND CLINICAL IMPLICATIONS

As noted at the outset of this chapter, there are limitations to available studies of interpersonal processes associated with depression, but one is nonetheless able to delineate what appears to be an important set of concerns, identify some key variables, and begin to appreciate the nature of the likely links between depression and relations with others. Still, the review is more a source of questions for future research than a source of definitive answers. Many limitations to the literature that was reviewed should be apparent. The existing literature does not begin to come to terms with heterogeneity in depression and the circumstances of depressed persons. There is minimal attention to even the basic distinction between unipolar and bipolar disorder. Further, although it is clear that some depressed persons do have harmonious and supportive relationships, there is little attention to what differences in their circumstances allow this to occur.

Finally, our lack of data concerning depression in men limits our ability to predict their response to conventional therapy for couples, and a highly flexible approach to them may be needed. Among options that might be considered are unilateral interventions for spouses that particularly target their negative involvement with their depressed partners (Watzlawick and Coyne 1980) and an approach to marital therapy that does not require conjoint sessions or enactment of problematic interactions (Coyne 1988). Finally, at the University of Michigan Depression Program, we are now experimenting with group interventions with spouses of depressed persons that combine psychoeducation with a structured approach to resolving their specific difficulties. One advantage of such an approach is that it does not depend on the patient's emergence from an episode to begin work on the couple's and family's difficulties.

REFERENCES

Arkowitz H, Holliday S, Hutter M: Depressed women and their husbands: a study of marital interaction and adjustment. Paper presented at the annual meeting of the Association for the Advancement of Behavioral Therapy, San Francisco, CA, November 1982

Beck AT: Cognitive Therapy and Emotional Disorders. New York, Guilford Press, 1976

Biglan A, Hops H, Sherman L, et al: Problem-solving interactions of depressed women and their husbands. Behavior Therapy 16:431–451, 1985

Biglan A, Hops H, Sherman L: Coercive family processes and maternal depression, in Marriages and Families: Behavioral Treatments and Processes. Edited by McMahon RJ, Peter RdeV. New York, Brunner/Mazel, 1988

Billings AG, Moos RH: Children of parents with unipolar depression: a controlled 1-year follow-up. J Abnorm Child Psychol 14:149–166, 1985

Birchnell J, Kennard J: Does marital maladjustment lead to mental illness? Soc Psychiatry 18:79–88, 1983

Blumberg SR, Hokanson JE: The effects of another person's response style on interpersonal behavior in depression. J Abnorm Psychol 92:196–209, 1983

Brown GW, Harris T (eds): Social Origins of Depression: A Study of Psychiatric Disorder in Women. New York, Free Press, 1978

Brown GW, Bifulco A, Harris T, et al: Life stress, chronic subclinical symptoms and vulnerability to clinical depression. J Affective Disord 11:1–19, 1986

Cleary PD, Kessler RC: The estimation and interpretation of modifier effects. J Health Soc Behav 23:159–168, 1982

Cohler BJ, Grunebaum HU, Weiss JL, et al: Child care attitudes and adaptation to the maternal role among mentally ill and well mothers. Am J Orthopsychiatry 46:123–133, 1977

Conners CK, Himmelhoch J, Goyette CH, et al: Children of parents with affective illness. J Am Acad Child Psychiatry 18:600–607, 1979

Courney RH: The effectiveness of attached social workers in the management of depressed female patients in general practice. Psychol Med 14 (Monogr suppl 6), 1984

Coyne JC: Toward an interactional description of depression. Psychiatry 39:28–40, 1976a

Coyne JC: Depression and the response of others. J Abnorm Psychol 2:186–193, 1976b

Coyne JC: Strategic therapy with couples having a depressed spouse, in Family Intervention in Affective Illness. Edited by Haas G, Glick I, Clarkin J. New York, Guilford Press, 1988

Coyne JC, DeLongis A: Going beyond social support: the role of social relationship in adaptation. J Consult Clin Psychol 54:454–460, 1986

Coyne JC, DeLongis A: The spouses of depressed persons. Unpublished manuscript, 1989

Coyne JC, Kahn J, Gotlib IH: Depression, in Family Interaction and Psychotherapy. Edited by Jacob T. New York, Plenum Press, 1987a

Coyne JC, Kessler RC, Tal M, et al: Living with a depressed person: burden and psychological distress. J Consult Clin Psychol 55:347–352, 1987b

Cytryn L, McKnew DH, Bartko JJ, et al: Offspring of patients with affective disorders II. J Am Acad Child Psychiatry 21:389–391, 1982

Decina P, Kestenbaum CJ, Farber S, et al: Clinical and psychological assessment of children of bipolar probands. Am J Psychiatry 140:548–553, 1983

Dolan RJ, Calloway SP, Fonagy P, et al: Life events, depression, and hypothalamic-pituitary-adrenal axis function. Br J Psychiatry 147: 429–433, 1985

Drake RE, Price JL: Depression: adaptation to disruption and loss. Perspect Psychiatr Care 13:163–169, 1975

Emery R, Weintraub S, Neale J: Effects of marital discord on the school behavior of children of schizophrenic, affectively disordered, and normal parents. J Abnorm Child Psychol 16:215–225, 1982

Epstein NB, Baldwin IM, Bishop DS: The McMaster assessment device. Journal of Marital and Family Therapy 9:171–180, 1983

Everitt BS, Smith AMR: Interaction in contingency tables: a brief description of alternative definitions. Psychol Med 9:581–583, 1979

Fisher L, Kokes RF, Harder DW, et al: Child competence and psychiatric risk, VI: summary and integration of findings. J Nerv Ment Dis 168:353–355, 1980

Fisher L, Kokes RF, Cole RE, et al: Competent children at risk: a study of well functioning offspring of disturbed parents, in The Invulnerable Child. Edited by Anthony EJ, Cohler BJ. New York, Guilford Press (in press)

Fowles DC, Gershon FS: Neurotic depression: the endogenous-reactive distinction, in The Psychobiology of Depressive Disorders. Edited by Depue RA. New York, Academic Press, 1979

Frey S, Jorns U, Daw WA: A systematic description and analysis of nonverbal interaction between doctors and patients in a psychiatric interview, in Ethology and Nonverbal Communication in Mental Health. Edited by Corson SA. New York, Pergamon Press, 1980

Friedman LS: Family interaction among children of unipolar depressed mothers: a naturalistic observation study. Unpublished doctoral dissertation, University of Oregon, Eugene, 1984

Gotlib IH, Robinson A: Responses to depressed individuals: discrepancies between self-report and observer-rated behavior. J Abnorm Psychol 91:231–240, 1982

Gurtman M: Depression and the response of others: reevaluating the reevaluation. J Abnorm Psychol 95:99–101, 1986

Hautzinger M, Linden M, Hoffman N: Distressed couples with and without a depressed partner: an analysis of their verbal interaction. J Behav Ther Exp Psychiatry 13:307–314, 1982

Herbert JD, Nelson RO, Herbert DL: The effects of feedback on the behavior of depressed inpatients in two structured interactions. Unpublished manuscript, 1988

Hinchliffe MK, Hopper D, Roberts FJ: The Melancholy Marriage. New York, Wiley, 1978

Hirsch BJ, Moos RF, Reischl TM: Psychosocial adjustment of adolescent children of a depressed, arthritic, or normal parent. J Abnorm Psychol 94:154–164, 1985

Hokanson JE, Sacco WP, Blumberg SR, et al: Interpersonal behavior of depressive individuals in a mixed-motive game. J Abnorm Psychol 89:320–332, 1980

Hooley JM, Orley J, Teasdale JD: Levels of expressed emotion and relapse in depressed patients. Br J Psychiatry 148:642–647, 1986

Hoover CF, Fitzgerald RG: Dominance in the marriage of affective patients. J Nerv Ment Dis 169:624–628, 1981

Jacobson NS, Schmelling KB, Salsalusky S, et al: Marital therapy as an adjunct treatment of depression. Paper presented at the annual meeting of the Association for the Advancement of Behavior Therapy, Boston, MA, 1987

Kahn J, Coyne JC, Margolin G: Depression and marital conflict: the social construction of despair. Journal of Social and Personal Relationships 2:447–462, 1985

Keitner GI, Miller IW, Epstein NB, et al: Family functioning and the course of major depression. Compr Psychiatry 28:54–64, 1987

Keller MB, Klerman GL, Lavori PW, et al: Long-term outcome of episodes of major depression: clinical and public health significance. JAMA 252:788–792, 1984

Kovacs M, Rush AJ, Beck AT, et al: Depressed outpatients treated with cognitive therapy or pharmacotherapy. Arch Gen Psychiatry 38:33–39, 1981

Kuyler PS, Rosenthal L, Igel G, et al: Psychopathology among children of manic depressive patients. Biol Psychiatry 15:589–597, 1980

Leff J, Vaughn CE: Expressed Emotion in Families: Its Significance for Mental Illness. New York, Guilford Press, 1985

Libet J, Lewinsohn PM: The concept of social skill with special reference to the behavior of depressed persons. J Consult Clin Psychol 40:304–312, 1973

McLean PD, Ogsten K, Grauer L: A behavioral approach to the treatment of depression. J Behav Ther Exp Psychiatry 4:323–330, 1973

Merikangas KR, Spiker DG: Assortative mating among inpatients with primary affective disorder. Psychol Med 12:753–764, 1982

Merikangas KR, Ranelli CJ, Kupfer DJ: Marital interaction in hospitalized depressed patients. J Nerv Ment Dis 167:689–695, 1979

Miller IW, Kabacoff RI, Keitner GI, et al: Family functioning in the families of psychiatric patients. Compr Psychiatry 27:302–312, 1986

Neale JM, Weintraub S: Children vulnerable to psychopathology: the Stony Brook High-Risk Project. J Abnorm Child Psychol 3:95–113, 1975

Negri F, Melica AM, Zuliani R, et al: Assortative mating and affective disorders. J Affective Disord 1:247–253, 1979

Parker G, Blignault I: Psychosocial predictors of outcomes in subjects with untreated depressive disorder. J Affective Disord 8:73–81, 1985

Parker G, Hadzi-Pavlovic D: Modification of levels of depression in mother-bereaved women by prenatal and marital relationships. Psychol Med 14:125–135, 1984

Parker G, Tennant C, Blignault I: Predicting improvement in patients with nonendogenous depression. Br J Psychiatry 146:132–139, 1985

Parker G, Holmes S, Manicavagar V: Depression in general practice attenders: caseness, natural history, and predictors of outcome. J Affective Disord 10:27–35, 1986

Patterson GR, Reid JB: Reciprocity and coercion: two facets of social systems, in Behavior Modification in Clinical Psychology. Edited by Neuringer C, Michael J. New York, Appleton-Century-Croft, 1970

Paykel ES: Causal relationships between clinical depression and life events, in Stress and Mental Disorder. Edited by Barrett JE. New York, Raven Press, 1979

Paykel ES, Myers JK, Dienelt MN, et al: Life events and depression: a controlled study. Arch Gen Psychiatry 21:753–757, 1969

Quinton D, Rutter M, Liddle C: Institutional rearing, parenting difficulties and marital support. Psychol Med 14:107–124, 1984

Rounsaville BJ, Weissman MM, Prusoff BA, et al: Marital disputes and treatment outcome in depressed women. Compr Psychiatry 20:483–490, 1979

Rounsaville BJ, Prusoff BA, Weissman MM: The course of marital disputes in depressed women: a 48-month follow-up study. Compr Psychiatry 21:111–118, 1980

Rush AJ, Shaw B, Khatami M: Cognitive therapy of depression: utilizing the couples system. Cognitive Therapy and Research 4:103–113, 1980

Sameroff AJ, Seifer R, Zax M: Early development of children at risk for emotional disorder. Monogr Soc Res Child Dev 47 (7), Serial No 199, 1982

Sameroff AJ, Barocas R, Seifer R: The early development of children born to mentally ill women, in Children at Risk for Schizophrenia. Edited by Watt NR, Anthony EJ, Wynne LC, et al. New York, Cambridge University Press, 1985

Seifer R, Sameroff AJ, Jones F: Adaptive behavior in young children of emotionally disturbed women. Journal of Developmental Psychology 1:251–276, 1981

Strack S, Coyne JC: Social confirmation of dysphoria: shared and private reactions to depression. J Pers Soc Psychol 44:806–814, 1983

Swann WB Jr, Predmore SC: Intimates as agents of social support: sources of consolation or despair? J Pers Soc Psychol 49:1609–1617, 1985

Vaughn CE, Leff J: The influence of family and social factors on the course of psychiatric illness. Br J Psychiatry 129:125–137, 1976

Watzlawick PW, Coyne JC: Depression following stroke: brief problem-focused family treatment. Fam Process 19:13–18, 1980

Weintraub S, Liebert D, Neale JM: Teacher ratings of children vulnerable to psychopathology, in The Child and His Family, Vol 14: Vulnerable Children. Edited by Anthony EJ. New York, Wiley, 1978, pp 335–346

Weissman MM, Paykel ES: The Depressed Woman. Chicago, IL, University of Chicago Press, 1974

Weissman MM, Kasl SV, Klerman GL: Follow-up of depressed women after maintenance treatment. Am J Psychiatry 133:757–760, 1976

Weissman MM, Prusoff BA, DeMascio A, et al: The efficacy of drugs and psychotherapy in the treatment of acute depressive episodes. Am J Psychiatry 136:555–558, 1979

Weissman MM, Klerman GL, Prusoff BA, et al: Depressed outpatients: results one year after treatment with drugs and/or interpersonal psychotherapy. Arch Gen Psychiatry 38:51–55, 1981

Weissman MM, Prusoff BA, Gammon GD, et al: Psychopathology in children (ages 6–18) of depressed and normal parents. J Am Acad Child Psychiatry 23:78–84, 1984

Yarkin KL, Harvey JH, Bloxom BM: Cognitive sets, attribution, and social interaction. J Pers Soc Psychol 41:243–252, 1981

Zahn-Waxler C, McKnew DH, Cummings EM, et al: Problem behaviors in peer interaction of young children with a manic-depressive parent. Am J Psychiatry 141:236–240, 1984

Chapter 3

Expressed Emotion and Depression

Jill M. Hooley, D.Phil.

Chapter 3

Expressed Emotion and Depression

Within the fields of psychiatry and psychopathology it is often the case that areas of research are prescribed more by the diagnostic groups on which they focus than by the constructs they investigate. Diagnostic boundaries therefore often limit the extent to which empirical findings associated with one diagnostic group will generate interest among those who work with other disordered populations.

From time to time, however, constructs associated with a particular psychiatric or psychological diagnosis transcend these conventional boundaries and become a source of interest to researchers and clinicians working in other areas. This chapter focuses on one such construct: expressed emotion, or EE. Research concerning the nature, origins, and sequelae of EE has, for some time, been a mainstay among researchers interested in relapse among schizophrenic persons. There is now growing evidence that this index of the family environment may also hold considerable potential for our understanding of relapse in depressed populations.

PSYCHOSOCIAL VARIABLES IN SCHIZOPHRENIA AND DEPRESSION RESEARCH

Recent developments in our understanding of the neurobiology of major mental disorders have been paralleled by a growing recognition of the importance of psychosocial factors in the development, main-

---

The research described in this chapter was supported by the Medical Research Council of the United Kingdom. Thanks are extended to Ruth Berkowitz and John Colvin for their assistance with reliability checks and to Kurt Hahlweg for help with the sequential analyses. The author is also grateful to John Orley for his independent assessments of patients' outcomes, to John Teasdale, and to John Richters, whose insightful comments on an early draft of this manuscript deserve special thanks.

tenance, and treatment of severe forms of psychopathology (Hahlweg and Goldstein 1987). In many respects, however, the psychosocial constructs that have become foci of attention for researchers interested in the affective disorders have not been the same constructs that have attracted the attention of schizophrenia researchers. Constructs such as marital adjustment and social support have been central to psychosocial research in mood disorders (inter alia Brown and Harris 1978; Bullock et al. 1972; Coleman and Miller 1975; Crowther 1985; Gotlib and Hooley 1988; Henderson 1981; Hinchliffe et al. 1978; Paykel et al. 1980; Paykel et al. 1969; Weissman and Paykel 1974). These variables, however, are less obviously woven into the pattern of psychosocial research in schizophrenia. Here, the construct of EE (see Hooley 1985 for a more detailed review) is a principal focus of attention. As I hope to show in this chapter, however, the difference between this construct and other constructs more familiar to depression researchers may be more apparent than real.

Expressed Emotion

Assessed during a 1- to 2-hour interview, the construct of EE reflects the extent to which a patient's closest relative(s) talks about him or her in a critical or hostile way, or in a way that reflects a dramatic or exaggerated response to the patient's illness. Relatives of schizophrenic patients who make six or more critical remarks and/or one hostile comment and/or show evidence of marked emotional overinvolvement are classified as high in EE. Relatives who fail to meet any of these three criteria are classified as low in EE.

As yet, it is by no means clear whether or to what extent these characteristics of relatives contribute to versus reflect poor functioning in patients. It is nonetheless impressive that several studies conducted in England and the United States have reported that schizophrenic patients who return home from the hospital to live with relatives characterized as high in EE have 9-month relapse rates that are several times higher than the relapse rates typical of patients living with low-EE family members (Brown et al. 1972; Karno et al. 1987; Vaughn and Leff 1976a; Vaughn et al. 1984). Moreover, data collected on samples of schizophrenic Mexican Americans (Jenkins et al. 1986) and schizophrenic persons living in Chandigarh, India (Leff et al. 1987), further suggest that, although proportions of high- and low-EE relatives vary across cultures, the EE-relapse link itself transcends cultural boundaries.

To date, almost all of the research on EE has focused on schizophrenic patient samples. However, an early schizophrenia study by Vaughn and Leff (1976a) also found an EE-relapse link in a comparison sample of unipolar depressed patients. Since then, however, perhaps because of the unfamiliarity of the EE construct and its strong ties to the literature on schizophrenia, the study of EE in the families of depressed patients has attracted little empirical attention.

This chapter provides a synthesis of the major findings from the only reported study to date that has attempted to replicate Vaughn and Leff's (1976a) findings in a sample of depressed patients and to extend the construct of EE to research on unipolar depressed patients. The chapter begins with a general introduction to the project, followed by an examination of its data concerning the EE-relapse link. Behavioral correlates of high and low levels of EE obtained during face-to-face interactions are then described, and previously unreported sequential analyses of interactions in both the high- and low-EE patient-relative dyads are presented. The association between EE and self-reports of relationship quality is then considered. Finally, data concerning the predictive validity of an alternative (and more easily measured) predictor of patients' relapse are described. The chapter ends with a consideration of the link between the constructs of EE and marital distress, as well as broader consideration of issues that are likely to form the focus of empirical work in the coming years.

THE OXFORD STUDY

The data discussed in this chapter derive from a longitudinal study of depressed inpatients and their spouses that was conducted at three psychiatric hospitals in and around Oxford, England. The aims of the investigation were to replicate and extend Vaughn and Leff's earlier work on EE in the families of depressed patients through 1) examination of the predictive validity of EE in another clinically depressed sample and 2) examination of the interactional correlates of high and low levels of EE in patient-spouse dyads. To this end, a sample of patients were recruited who met Present State Examination (PSE) criteria (Wing et al. 1974) and Research Diagnostic Criteria (RDC) (Spitzer et al. 1978) for major depressive disorder, who were aged between 20 and 70 years, and who were currently living with a marital partner. Patients with suspected organic illness or psychotic symptoms were excluded. All of the 42 inpatients who participated in the study were recruited during their hospital admission and assessed by interviewers who had been trained in the administration and scoring of the PSE. Inter-rater agreement among these raters with respect to whether patients met clinical criteria for major depression was 100%.

A total of 39 patients (23 women, 16 men) were successfully

followed up for 9 months subsequent to their return to their families. During this time, they received two PSE interviews, which took place at 3 and 9 months after hospital discharge and were conducted by an independent psychiatrist who was blind to the spouses' EE levels. The typical depressed patient who participated in the project was 48 years old (range 27–70 years) and had been married for over 20 years. Couples had a mean number of two children and tended to come primarily from lower-middle-class or working-class backgrounds. Beck Depression Inventory (Beck et al. 1961) scores averaged 25 for the patients (SD = 10.4) and 6 for their spouses (SD = 3.8).

EE in the Spouses of Depressed Patients

During the patients' initial period of hospitalization, all spouses were interviewed (in the absence of the patient) with the Camberwell Family Interview (CFI; Vaughn and Leff 1976b). On the basis of the comments made during this audiotaped interview, levels of criticism, hostility, and emotional overinvolvement in the patients' spouses were assessed. Measures of warmth and frequency of positive remarks about the patient are also derived from the CFI. However, because previous research has indicated that these variables do not predict relapse in schizophrenic samples, they do not form part of the EE index.

An examination of EE scale scores revealed two findings particularly worthy of mention. First, wives of depressed men made many more critical remarks about their depressed husbands than did the husbands of the depressed women (10.5 vs. 5.8 critical comments, $P < .01$). CFI data also suggested that high levels of emotional overinvolvement (a rating of 3 or more on a 6-point scale) are extremely rare—at least in the spouses of depressed patients. Only 3 (2 wives and 1 husband) of the 42 spouses interviewed evidenced levels of emotional overinvolvement high enough to warrant classification as high EE on the basis of this measure alone. Two of these 3 spouses were also rated as being extremely critical. There was therefore only 1 spouse who qualified for a high-EE rating on the basis of emotional overinvolvement alone. Interestingly, the wife of this man was also the only patient to withdraw from the study during the follow-up period. All spouses of patients for whom relapse data are available are thus rated as high-EE on the basis of the number of critical remarks they made during the EE interview.

Table 1 shows the intercorrelations among the five CFI variables rated during the EE interview. As expected, criticism and hostility are positively correlated and are negatively associated with warmth.

remark's verbal content. It is thus possible (although rare) for negative verbal behaviors to receive positive nonverbal qualifiers and for positive verbal remarks to be coded as being accompanied by negative nonverbal behavior.

Reliability. All videotaped interactions were coded by the author, who at the time the ratings were made was blind to the EE statuses of the spouses. A second individual, also blind to relatives' EE levels, independently coded 2 hours of randomly selected interactions in order to provide reliability checks. Levels of inter-rater agreement for the positive, negative, and neutral summary codes were high (kappa = .81) across the two coders. The individual codes of Criticism, Agreement, Self-disclosure, Acceptance, and Negative Solution also showed high levels of inter-rater agreement (Pearson's r_s = .83–.98). The verbal codes of Justification and Positive Solution, however, perhaps because of their low frequencies of occurrence, were not reliable enough to warrant inclusion into the analysis (r = .64 and r = .60, respectively). Because Positive Solution was unreliable, its reliable negative counterpart (Negative Solution) was also dropped from further investigation. Analyses were thus conducted using the three verbal summary codes (positive, negative, and neutral), the five individual verbal codes (Criticism, Disagreement, Agreement, Acceptance, and Self-disclosure), and the three nonverbal codes (positive, negative, and neutral)—all of which showed high levels of inter-rater agreement (kappa = .81; Pearson's r_s = .91–.96).

Behavior during the interaction. The results of the videotaping study provide evidence for the concurrent validity of EE in the spouses of depressed patients. Paralleling their behavior in the CFI, high-EE spouses[2] directed higher frequencies of criticism toward the patients with whom they interacted than did their low-EE counterparts (1.06 vs. 0.00, $P < .001$). High-EE spouses were also more likely to disagree with what patients said to them than were spouses rated low in EE (8.4 vs. 4.9, $P < .05$).

The third behavioral difference between the high- and low-EE spouses was revealed when the KPI category of verbal acceptance was considered: compared with low-EE spouses, high-EE spouses were much less accepting of patients (2.8 vs. 7.0, $P < .05$). In other words, they were less likely to make remarks that indicated that they considered the patient's point of view to be worthwhile or valid.

The nonverbal characteristics of the high-EE spouses were also remarkably congruent with their verbal behaviors. Although negative nonverbal behaviors made up only 2% of the nonverbal behavior demonstrated by low-EE spouses, 18% of the utterances coded for

Table 2. KPI verbal categories

Category	Example
POSITIVE	
Self-disclosure	
Expression of feelings	I'm too angry to listen.
Expression of wishes	I'd like to go away this weekend.
Positive Solution	
Constructive proposals	Let me take the kids to school tomorrow.
Compromises	I'll cook dinner if you'll do the dishes.
Acceptance	
Paraphrases	You're saying that you think the kids are too young to be left alone.
Open questions	Are you feeling better?
Positive feedback	I liked the way you did that.
Empathy/concern	Things will improve soon.
Agreement	
Direct agreement	Yes, that's right.
Acceptance of responsibility	I know, it was my fault.
Assent	Yes, Fine, or OK.
NEUTRAL	
Problem Description	
Neutral description	The kids aren't doing well at school.
Neutral question	Did you have trouble with the car today?
Metacommunication	
Clarification	Say that again, please.
Topic tracking	We're getting away from the real issue.
Irrelevant Utterances	Inaudible statements; remarks that do not fit any category.
NEGATIVE	
Criticism	
Specific	You didn't talk to me at all during dinner.
Personal	You are lazy!
Negative Solution	We'd be able to save more if you didn't drive such a big car.

Table 2. KPI verbal categories—Continued

Category	Example
Justification	
Excuse	I couldn't go because I was too busy yesterday.
Denial of responsibility	That's not my job anyway.
Disagreement	
Direct	No, you're wrong.
Yes-but	Yes, you're right but we don't have the money.
Short	No.
Blocking	That's it. I've had enough.

Note. Reprinted from Hooley JM: Expressed emotion and depression: interactions between patients and high- versus low-expressed-emotion spouses. J Abnorm Psychol 95:237–246, 1986. Copyright 1986 by the American Psychological Association. Reprinted by permission of the publisher and author. KPI = Kategoriensystem für Partnerschaftlische Interaktion.

high-EE spouses were assigned negative nonverbal qualifiers ($P < .01$). There was also a difference in production of positive nonverbal cues. Although positive nonverbal behaviors accounted for more than half of the low-EE spouses' total nonverbal behavior, only 37% of the nonverbal behaviors emitted by high-EE spouses were rated as positive ($P < .05$). Percentages of neutral nonverbal behavior, however, did not differ across the high- and low-EE groupings.

Taken together, these findings indicate that the behaviors of high-EE relatives differ from those found among low-EE relatives of depressed patients in a number of important respects. However, it is important to note that differences between the interactions of high- and low-EE dyads do not result only from differences in the behavior of the spouses: a number of variables also discriminated between high- and low-EE patients.[3] Like the spouses with whom they interacted, high-EE patients made fewer positive verbal statements than patients who had low-EE marital partners ($P < .05$). In large measure, this is because they made significantly fewer self-disclosing remarks (4.8 vs. 8.2, $P < .01$).

Also of interest is patients' nonverbal behavior. Compared with patients who have low-EE spouses, depressed partners of high-EE spouses were much more neutral with respect to the nonverbal behavior they exhibited. Almost 60% of the verbal statements made by high-EE patients were accompanied by neutral nonverbal behavior. Patients who interacted with low-EE partners, on the other hand, were neutral on only 42% of their verbal comments ($P < .05$). Because patients in the high- and the low-EE groups did not differ with respect to their Beck Depression Inventory scores, differences in severity of clinical condition do not appear to provide a good explanation for these findings.

Sequential Analysis of High- and Low-EE Interactions

Identification of differences in the frequencies of behaviors across high- and low-EE dyads is an important first step in understanding the nature of relationships that are marked by different levels of EE. Frequency analyses are most valuable, however, when they are accompanied by information about the sequencing of behaviors across time. In the section below, we consider two questions that hold the potential to shed light on the dynamics of high- and low-EE relationships: 1) Do high- and low-EE couples show different *patterns* of behavior during face-to-face interactions? 2) Within each type of dyad, who is more responsible for keeping the escalation process going?

K-Gramm analysis. The patterning of the interactions of the high- and low-EE dyads was examined using a technique called K-Gramm analysis (Revenstorf et al. 1984). This method of sequential analysis (developed by the same team of researchers that produced the KPI) examines real but generalized behavior patterns. With the K-Gramm method, data are summed across couples (boundaries between couples are preserved), and the data set is then scanned for behavioral sequences of a particular length. At the 1-gramm level, the relative probability of a particular behavior is assessed. This level is therefore analogous to the frequency or base rate data described above. A 2-gramm analysis, on the other hand, assesses the conditional probability of x given y, whereas at the 3-gramm level, the probability of z given x and y is under investigation.

One advantage of K-Gramm analysis is that the behavior chains it examines are genuine sequences of behavior. In this respect, it differs from lag sequential analysis (Sackett 1977), which takes no account of the behaviors that occur between an antecedent behavior and its lagged response. K-Gramm analysis thus provides a more accurate portrayal of couples' interactions. However, one problem encountered within K-Gramm analysis is that the size of the available data set decreases as the length of the sequence increases. This is because few couples show very long chains of particular behaviors.

To minimize this problem and to increase the overall reliability of the analysis, the four positive and four negative verbal codes of the KPI were collapsed into two categories. The first of these—Positive Communication—comprised the KPI codes Agreement, Acceptance, Self-disclosure, and Positive Solution. The second reduction category, termed Negative Communication, was made up from the negative KPI codes of Criticism, Disagreement, Justification, and Negative Solution. EE groupings derived from a median-split procedure were also used to make the numbers of high- and low-EE dyads as similar as possible.

The second problem associated with K-Gramm analysis is less easily dealt with. Because of the aggregation across couples, statistical analyses of the differences between the high- and low-EE groups are not considered possible (Revenstorf et al. 1984; Revenstorf et al. 1980). The results of K-Gramm analyses must therefore be interpreted descriptively. Exploratory findings are offered here in the hope that they may help shed some light on the dynamics of high- and low-EE relationships within depressed samples.

Positive and negative escalation. Of particular interest in the analysis of couples' interactions are sequences of positive and negative communication behaviors. Examples of the former, which will be referred to as positive escalation, involve an alternating and reciprocal pattern of positive communication (e.g., PC-PC-PC-PC). Because individual behavior codes are collapsed to generate these summary codes, positive communication sequences might involve any combination of the four positive KPI codes. For example, partner A makes a self-disclosing remark. This is followed by an agreement from partner B. This stimulates another self-disclosure by A, which prompts B to respond with an accepting comment. Negative escalation, in contrast, involves a sequence of negative communications. Each partner responds to the other's negative communications by being negative in return. For example, partner A might make a remark that is critical of partner B. B may respond to this with a statement justifying his or her own behavior. If A subsequently disagrees with this justification, B may reply with a remark that is critical of A. Only if A does not respond to this with yet another negative behavior, but instead says something neutral or even positive (e.g., "You are right. It was wrong of me to say that"), is the negative escalation sequence considered ended at a sequence length of four.

To examine escalation patterns, data from all couples are combined. The data set is then searched for sequences of a particular length (e.g., chains of five negative behaviors in succession). At each K-Gramm level, the size of the available data set is therefore reduced. This is because sequences of six negative behaviors must be drawn from couples who produce sequences of five negative behaviors. Conditional probabilities show the likelihood of another negative (or positive) behavior being produced at each point in the sequential chain.

Escalation Patterns in High- and Low-EE Couples

Figure 1 shows the positive verbal escalation processes typical of high- and low-EE dyads.[4] The conditional probability [*P* (x/x)] is given on the ordinate; sequence length appears on the abscissa. Sequence length 1 represents the base rates of positive verbal behavior in both groups. Examination of the figure reveals that about 40% of all the verbal behavior within high-EE dyads is positive. This is in contrast to an overall frequency of 53% positive behavior in low-EE couples. As is already clear from the frequency analyses presented

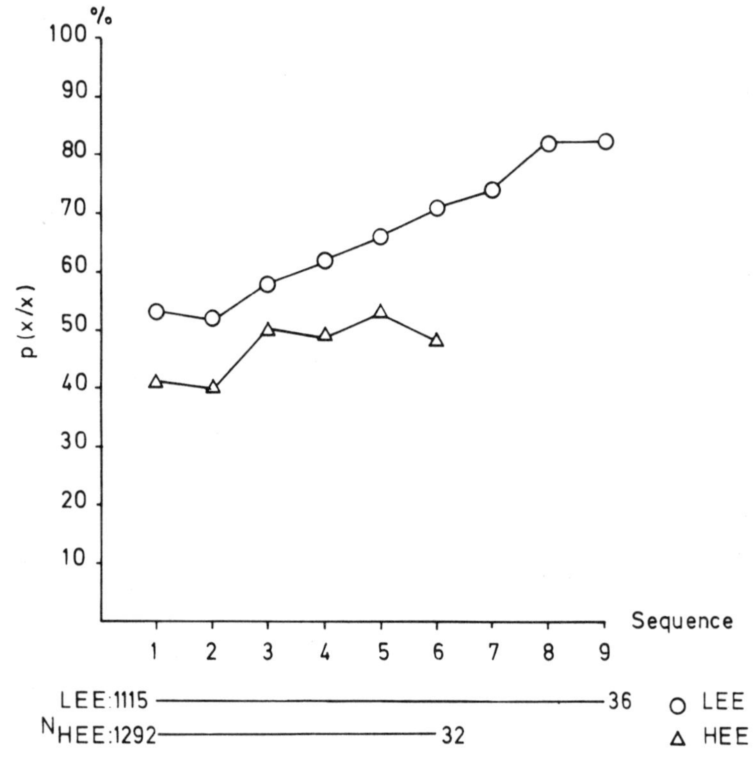

Figure 1. Positive verbal escalation in high–expressed emotion (HEE) and low–expressed emotion (LEE) dyads.

above, this difference in the base rates of positive verbal behavior across high- and low-EE dyads is largely due to differences between the high- and low-EE spouses.

Examination of the escalation patterns of low-EE dyads indicates that if partner A shows positive behavior, the probability that partner B will respond positively is .53. Given that B responds in this way, the probability is then .57 that A will again be positive and .62 that B will again reciprocate. The pattern of positive escalation ends at a maximum sequence length of 9 due to lack (or low probability of occurrence) of any sequences with a length of 10. The figure 36 written underneath sequence length 9 indicates that a chain of 9 positive verbal communications was observed 36 times in the low-EE group as a whole.

Figure 1 indicates that couples in the high-EE group also showed some positive verbal escalation—albeit at a lower probability than the low-EE dyads. The high-EE dyads also failed to maintain the escalation sequence for as long as the low-EE couples. No sequences with a length of more than 6 were found in the high-EE data set.

A similar pattern of interaction is obtained when positive nonverbal behavior is examined (Figure 2). Low-EE couples have higher initial probabilities of positive nonverbal behavior (.45 vs. .30), reach a

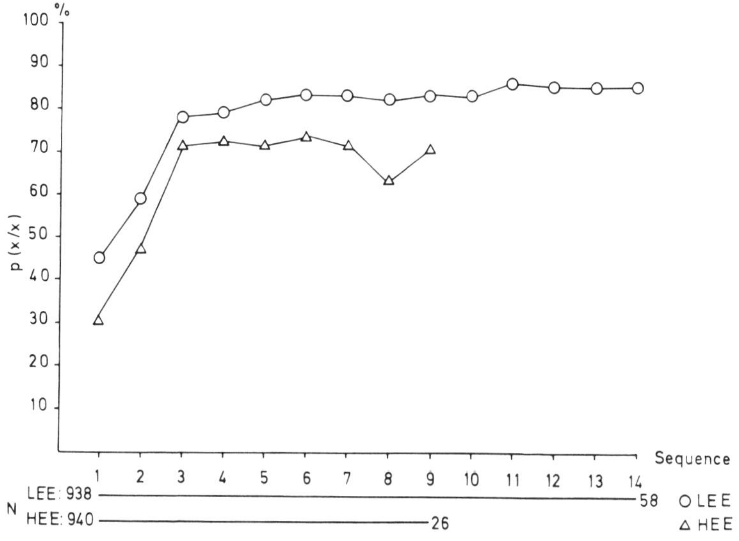

Figure 2. Positive nonverbal escalation in high–expressed emotion (HEE) and low–expressed emotion (LEE) dyads.

higher maximum probability level (.85 vs. .73), and continue the positive interaction sequence for longer than their high-EE counterparts (sequence length 14 vs. 9).

For the negative escalation process, the opposite is true (Figure 3). Here it is the high-EE dyads that show the most clear-cut escalations. Not only do these couples begin at higher levels of negative

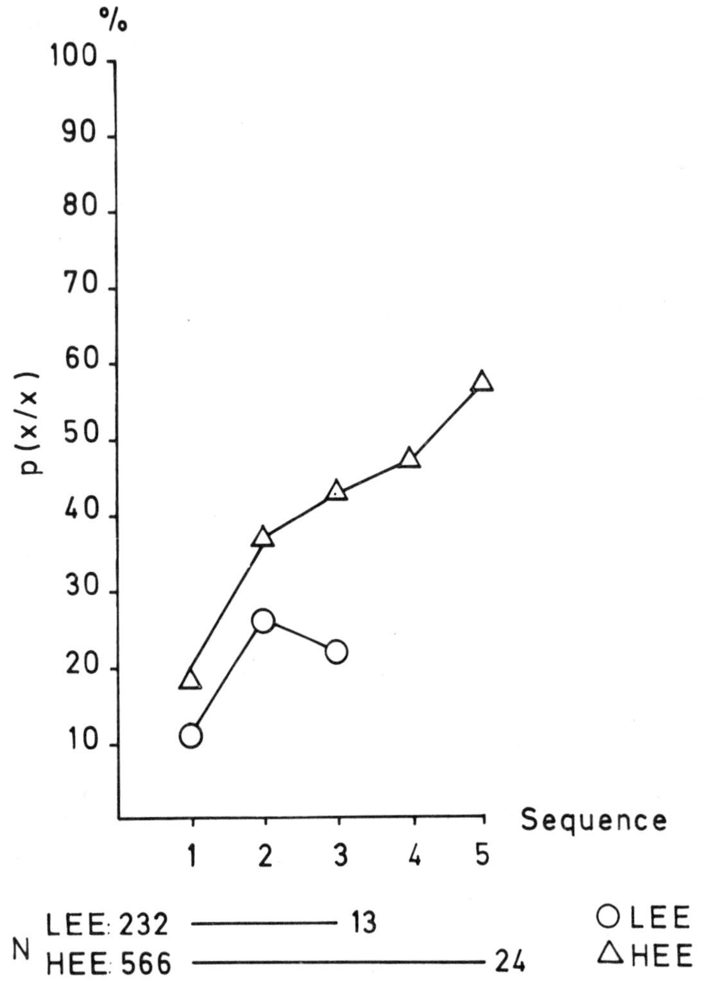

Figure 3. Negative verbal escalation in high–expressed emotion (HEE) and low–expressed emotion (LEE) dyads.

verbal behavior than low-EE couples, but they also continue the negative interaction sequence for longer. Low-EE couples, on the other hand, do not show a tendency to negatively escalate. Indeed, they appear to rapidly de-escalate after their partner has reciprocated negatively. Thus, although in high-EE couples the probability of negative behavior at sequence length 3 is higher than the corresponding probability at sequence length 2, this is not the case in low-EE couples. In these couples, the probability of negative behavior at sequence length 3 is lower than the probability of negative behavior at sequence length 2.

Differences between the interaction patterns of high- and low-EE dyads become even more striking when nonverbal negative escalation patterns are examined. As is apparent from Figure 4, low-EE couples show no negative nonverbal escalation at all. This is in sharp contrast to high-EE couples, who rapidly escalate to a high level (>.70) and

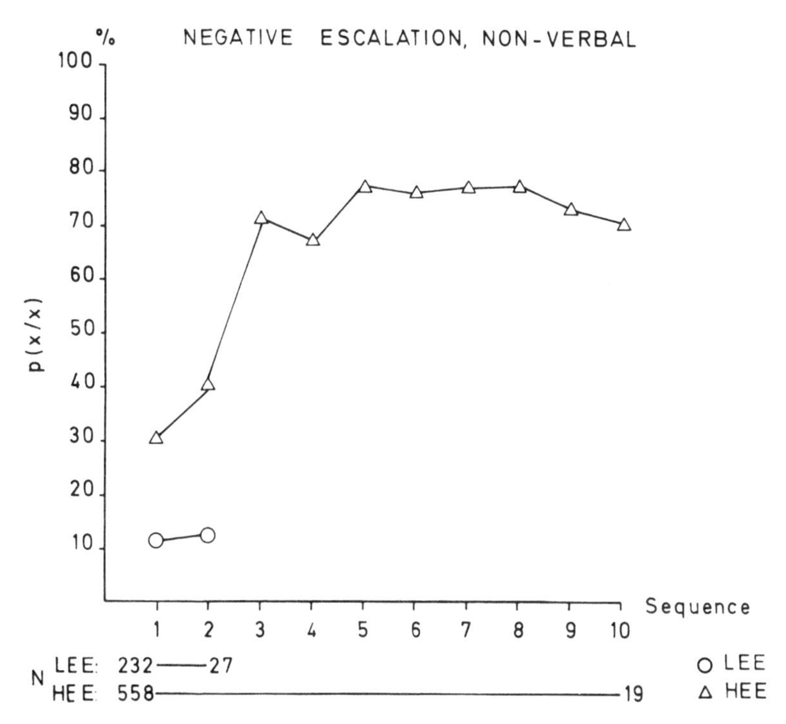

Figure 4. Negative nonverbal escalation in high–expressed emotion (HEE) and low–expressed emotion (LEE) dyads.

continue the negative exchange for an extended sequence (sequence length 10).

Who Is Responsible for Keeping the Escalation Sequence Going?

In the analyses just described, no account was taken of the individual (patient or spouse) who initiated a particular interaction sequence. To examine responsibility for maintaining interactions, positive and negative escalation processes were therefore reanalyzed according to whether the patient or the spouse began each particular type of interaction.

Figure 5 shows the positive verbal escalation process in high- and low-EE couples. It is apparent from this figure that, although the probability of initiating a positive escalation sequence was lower for

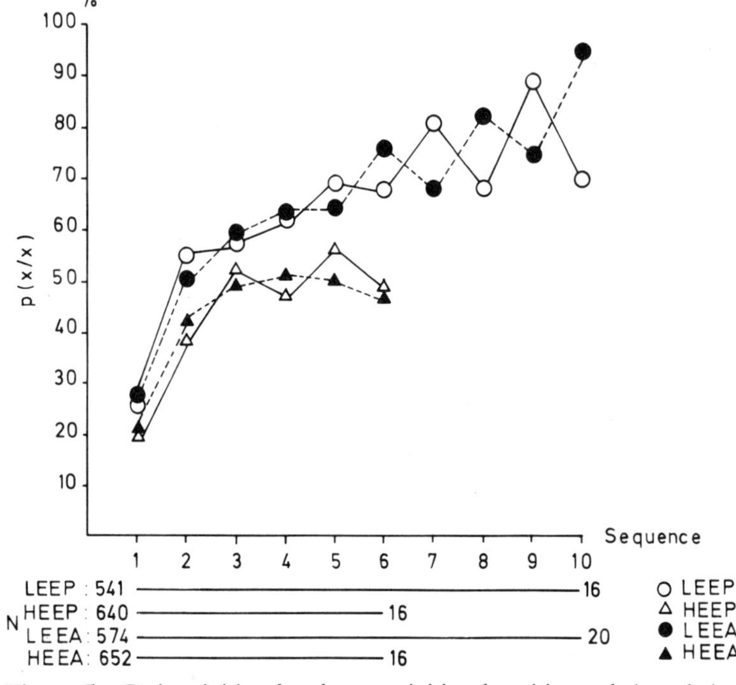

Figure 5. Patient-initiated and spouse-initiated positive verbal escalation sequences in high– and low–expressed emotion (EE) dyads. *Open symbols* denote interactions initiated by spouses; *closed symbols* denote interactions initiated by patients. LEEP = low-EE patients; HEEP = high-EE patients; LEEA = low-EE spouses; HEEA = high-EE spouses.

high-EE couples, within dyad types (high or low EE) the probability of a positive escalation sequence being initiated by a patient was very similar to the probability of a positive escalation sequence being initiated by a spouse. It is also clear that, up to a sequence length of 5 or 6, no marked differences between patient-initiated and spouse-initiated sequences are apparent. At sequence length 6, however, an oscillation pattern becomes apparent in the low-EE couples. Regardless of who begins the sequence, after sequence length 6, patients with low-EE dyads always show a higher conditional probability of reacting positively to the spouse than the spouses themselves show in response to the patients.[5]

When the data for nonverbal positive escalation are examined (Figure 6), this pattern becomes even more pronounced. Up to a

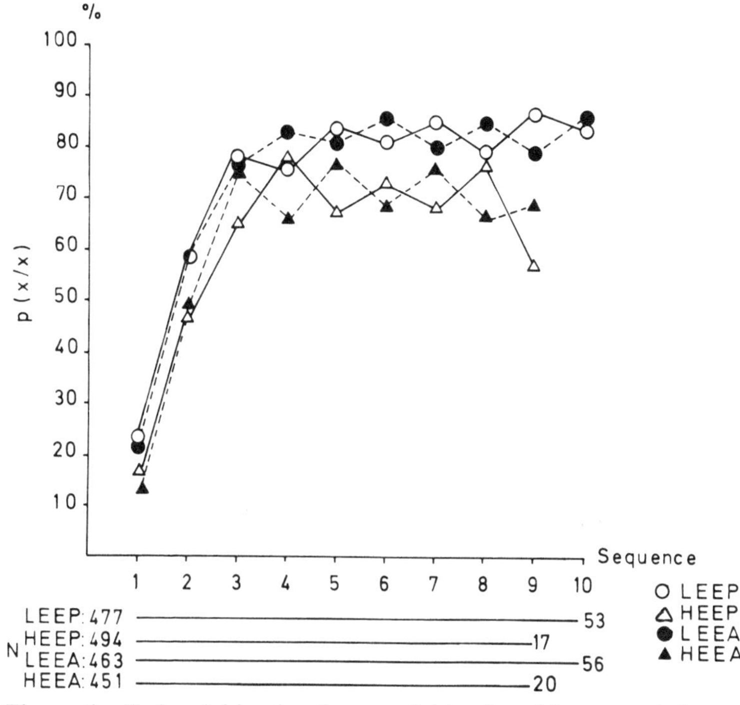

Figure 6. Patient-initiated and spouse-initiated positive nonverbal escalation sequences in high– and low–expressed emotion (EE) dyads. *Open symbols* denote interactions initiated by spouses; *closed symbols* denote interactions initiated by patients. LEEP = low-EE patients; HEEP = high-EE patients; LEEA = low-EE spouses; HEEA = high-EE spouses.

sequence length of 2 (high EE) or 4 (low EE), no differences in the conditional probabilities of responding for patients and spouses are apparent. After these points, however, oscillation processes begin. Regardless of who initiated the sequence, within low-EE dyads the probability of the patient remaining positive is always greater than the probability of the spouse remaining positive. In high-EE dyads the converse is true—the probability of the spouse remaining positive is always higher than the probability of the patient remaining positive. This suggests that in low-EE dyads it is the patients who are actively encouraging their spouses to remain in the positive interaction sequences. Within high-EE dyads, in contrast, it is the spouses who adopt this role. A similar pattern is also observed when negative escalation patterns are examined. In the interest of economy of space, however, the escalation plots are not depicted here.

Precisely what these differences in the dynamics of high- and low-EE interactions mean, however, is not clear. Although the developers of the K-Gramm system typically equate higher probabilities of responding with greater control of the interaction, others (e.g., Gottman 1979) have argued that the dominant individual is the individual whose behavior is *least* predictable. It is perhaps prudent therefore to refrain from making premature conclusions about these data at this time and turn instead to a consideration of the link between EE and marital distress.

EE and Marital Satisfaction

The results presented thus far suggest that relationships involving a high-EE partner differ from relationships involving a low-EE partner in several important ways. Some of these differences are quantitative and can be seen in the behavior of both the high-EE spouses and the depressed patients with whom they interact. Other differences, such as low-EE couples' tendencies to avoid or rapidly curtail negative escalation sequences, appear more qualitative in nature. Taken together, however, the data suggest that all is not well within high-EE relationships.

It is therefore no surprise to discover that the marriages of high-EE dyads are indeed more distressed than the marital relationships of low-EE dyads (Hooley and Hahlweg 1986). Analyses of Dyadic Adjustment Scale (DAS) scores (Spanier 1976) obtained during the patients' hospitalization revealed that the mean DAS score for patients living with low-EE spouses was 111.6,[6] compared to a mean DAS score of 97.4 obtained from patients living with high-EE marital partners ($P < .05$). Similar results are obtained when the mean marital satisfaction ratings of the spouses are examined (low-EE spouses

113.6, high-EE spouses 99.2; $P < .01$). The marital satisfaction ratings of both patients and spouses were also significantly correlated with the frequency of critical remarks made by spouses during the EE interview ($r_{34} = -.47, P < .005$ for patients; $r_{34} = -.32, P < .05$ for spouses). These findings raise the interesting possibility that patients' ratings of marital satisfaction may provide a convenient predictor of symptom relapse in depressed samples.

Marital Satisfaction as a Predictor of Relapse

Levels of EE reflect the extent to which relatives of psychiatric patients speak about patients in negative or emotionally overinvolved ways. The fact that there are significant correlations between spouses' criticism levels and ratings of marital quality obtained from spouses and patients, however, suggests that the EE interview may be telling us more about the patient-spouse *relationship* than it is about the spouses per se.

To test the possibility that measures of marital satisfaction and measures of EE may be functionally equivalent predictors of relapse in depressed patients, a series of hierarchically organized logistic regression analyses were conducted (Hooley and Teasdale, in press). In these analyses, the order of entry of predictor variables (spouses' criticism and patients' DAS scores) was systematically manipulated. Before the entry of any variables, however, Beck Depression Inventory scores (which were not predictive of relapse) were entered into the equation to control for differences in severity of patients' clinical conditions.

The results were most interesting. Addition of either spouses' criticism or patients' DAS scores into the regression equation led to a significant increase in the predictive power of the model. Entry of one variable subsequent to the entry of the other, however, rendered the contribution of the second predictor redundant. This was the case regardless of whether EE or DAS was entered into the equation first. Both variables are thus significantly associated with patients' relapse rates. However, information about one variable obviates the need for information about the other. These results suggest that, in married samples at least, EE in spouses' and patients' self-reports of marital quality are interchangeable predictors of depressive relapse. Further investigation also revealed that the two variables account for approximately the same proportion of the variance in depressive outcome (14 and 13%, respectively).

Given the tremendous difference in the cost of obtaining the two measures, this is a potentially important finding. The CFI takes at least 1 hour to administer and 2–3 hours to code and must be coded by an individual who has received several weeks of formal training. The DAS, in contrast, can be completed by most patients in 5–10 minutes. The finding that DAS scores predict patients' relapse as well as EE ratings thus has considerable practical as well as theoretical interest.

Patients' Perceptions of Spouses' Criticism

More easily obtained and even more strongly predictive of patients' relapse in this sample, however, was patients' response to the simple question, How critical is your spouse of you? This question was added to the end of the DAS and completed by 23 patients. Responses were rated using a 1–10 scale (1 = not at all critical, 10 = very critical indeed). Although it only took patients a matter of seconds to provide these ratings of perceived criticism, the results indicate that this is a variable that may be of considerable interest to those concerned with the rapid identification of patients at high risk for relapse.

The correlation between perceived criticism and patients' relapse was .64. The more critical a patient rated his or her spouse, the more likely that patient was to relapse over the 9-month follow-up period. When first entered into the logistic regression analyses described above, patients' perceptions of spouses' criticism accounted for over 40% of the variance in depressive relapse rates. Even with DAS and/or EE in the regression equation, entry of perceived criticism was still able to account for a significant increase in the variance left unexplained. When entered into the model first, perceived criticism rendered the subsequent contributions of both EE and DAS redundant.

Importantly, patients' ratings of spouses' criticism were not associated with gender. Neither were they correlated with severity of depression: there was no significant association between perceived criticism and patients' Beck Depression Inventory scores ($r_{23} = .02$). Still more interesting is the finding that patients' perceived criticism scores remained stable across illness and recovery periods. Test-retest reliability between admission and 3-month follow-up is high [$r_{(18)} = .75$]. It is also comparable to the 3-month test-retest reliability of perceived criticism ratings (how critical is your spouse [i.e., the patient] of you) obtained from patients' spouses. These individuals were nondepressed on both occasions. Within the perceived criticism rating, we thus have a measure that is 1) much more easily obtained than ratings of EE or marital satisfaction and 2) much more strongly associated with patients' rates of relapse. There is now an obvious need for an independent replication of these findings in a larger sample of patients.

SUMMARY AND SUGGESTIONS FOR FUTURE RESEARCH

The results presented in this chapter demonstrate the predictive validity of the EE construct in clinically depressed samples. Unipolar patients who live with critical or high-EE spouses are significantly more likely to relapse within a 9-month period after hospital discharge than are patients who live with noncritical or low-EE spouses. A recent demonstration of a link between EE and relapse in manic patients (Miklowitz et al. 1987) further suggests that the construct may be important not only for our understanding of depression, but for our understanding of affective disorders more generally.

However, it is also important to keep in mind that the EE-relapse link is still poorly understood. If the early promise of EE research is to be fulfilled, future studies will need to subject the EE construct to more penetrating (and more critical) scrutiny. In the following section, I shall focus on a number of specific questions that are raised by the data presented in this chapter.

What Is Being Measured?

EE most commonly is considered to reflect characteristics of relatives (Vaughn 1986). The interactional data described above, however, seriously question the validity of this assumption. Certainly, the behavior of high-EE spouses is very different from the behavior of low-EE spouses. However, as the data presented in this chapter demonstrate, there are also potentially important differences in the behavior of the patients with whom these high- and low-EE spouses interact. The question of who is reacting to whom thus becomes of central importance. It is by no means clear, for example, whether the unexpressive behaviors found in depressed patients interacting with high-EE spouses are a consequence of their spouses' criticism or a cause of it, or reflect a more complex interaction between patient and relative factors.

This issue strikes to the very heart of interpretations of the EE-relapse link. Many implicitly assume that the association between relatives' EE levels and patients' relapse rates is a causal one from relative to patient. However, it remains equally possible that subtle characteristics of patients 1) engender high levels of criticism in family members and 2) are themselves associated (for other reasons) with a relatively poor prognosis. If this is the case, high levels of EE might simply serve as a marker for those patients at highest risk for relapse.

It also remains possible—and perhaps most likely—that patient and relative factors interact. Within this formulation, patient characteristics are viewed as engendering negative responses only in some types of individuals. These negative or high-EE responses can then be viewed as causally related to relapse.

High levels of EE have been found not to be related to such patient characteristics as severity of illness (Brown et al. 1972; Hooley et al. 1986; Miklowitz et al. 1983; Vaughn et al. 1984) and levels of premorbid adjustment (Miklowitz et al. 1983). However, a wide range of other patient characteristics still remain to be investigated. In the absence of more detailed investigations designed to examine possible patient-related factors associated with differences in high and low family levels of EE, the relative merits of these three competing explanations of the EE-relapse link cannot be evaluated satisfactorily. The point here, however, is not to argue for the merits of one model over the other. Rather, it is to emphasize that common causal assumptions about the EE-relapse link are false comforts unless they can survive rigorous empirical tests of competing models. The possibility that levels of EE may be marking real differences between the patients and/or differences within the patient-relative interaction system as a whole clearly deserves much more empirical attention than it has received to date.

Are High Levels of EE Marking Distressed Relationships?

The putative link between EE and relationship distress also warrants further consideration. In this sample at least, EE and marital satisfaction appear to be interchangeable predictors of relapse. The interaction patterns typical of high- and low-EE dyads also show striking similarities to the interaction patterns typical of distressed and nondistressed couples (inter alia Billings 1979; Gottman et al. 1977; Hahlweg et al. 1984b; Koren et al. 1980). An obvious next step for researchers in this area is therefore to examine the effects of marital therapy on high levels of EE.

In short, we must be open to the possibility that EE may simply be old wine in new bottles. The construct that has served schizophrenia research well over the last two decades may, in the final analysis, be little more than an alternative measure of relationship quality. And, if the results presented here can be replicated in new samples, it will suggest that the expensive and time-consuming procedures for assessing EE may add little to the predictive and explanatory power of relationship measures that are more easily obtained. If future empirical studies replicate the relapse findings presented in this chapter using self-reports of the quality of the family relationships of unmarried schizophrenic patients, a rethinking of the nature of the EE construct may be in order.

Is There a Better Predictor of Relapse?

Although this is a simple question, it currently has no simple answer. However, the perceived criticism data discussed above do raise the possibility that ratings obtained from patients about how critical their family members are may provide a potentially important predictor of psychiatric relapse. Certainly these ratings outpredicted the EE measure in the current depressed sample. We are now investigating whether the perceived criticism ratings that schizophrenic patients make about their relatives predict relapse as well as the perceived criticism ratings depressed patients make about their family members.

CONCLUDING REMARKS

Although issues of causality currently make the EE-relapse link difficult to interpret, the contribution that the construct has made to research on psychosocial factors in psychopathology should not be underestimated. There is little doubt that EE is a reliable and robust predictor of relapse in schizophrenic and affectively disordered patients. Interest in EE has also led to the development of a number of successful techniques for intervention in the families of psychiatric patients (Anderson et al. 1980; Falloon et al. 1982; Falloon et al. 1984; Hogarty et al. 1986; Leff et al. 1982). In an area of research plagued by Type I errors and failures to replicate, EE research provides a potentially important first step toward a better understanding of psychiatric relapse.

It is, however, only a first step. The EE-relapse link remains an important body of data in search of an explanation. Moreover, it is becoming increasingly clear that further demonstrations of the EE-relapse link will have little value unless they are couched within broader efforts to gain a process-level understanding of psychiatric relapse. The next few years will be an important time for research in this area. Within a general climate of optimism about the value of the construct, the time is now ripe for a detailed examination of what have always been the most important questions facing EE researchers: What is EE and why is it associated with psychiatric relapse?

NOTES

1. Not all couples managed to interact for 15 minutes. To avoid unnecessary loss of subjects, the data reported here concern the first 10 minutes of the interaction.
2. A median split (total - sample median = seven critical comments) was used to assign spouses to the high- and low-EE groups. Very similar results are obtained when a cutoff of three critical remarks is used (see Hooley 1986).
3. For the sake of convenience, patients with high-EE spouses are referred to as high-EE patients; patients with low-EE spouses are referred to as low-EE patients.
4. Within these analyses, no distinction is made between sequences initiated by patients and sequences initiated by spouses.
5. Within escalation processes initiated by patients, data points 2, 4, 6, etc., reflect probabilities for spouses, whereas data points 1, 3, 5, etc., reflect probabilities for patients. The converse is true for escalation processes initiated by spouses.
6. These EE groupings are again derived from a median split.

REFERENCES

Anderson CM, Hogarty GE, Reiss DJ: Family treatment of adult schizophrenic patients: a psychoeducational approach. Schizophr Bull 6:490–505, 1980

Beck AT, Ward CH, Mendelsohn M, et al: An inventory for measuring depression. Arch Gen Psychiatry 4:561–571, 1961

Billings A: Conflict resolution in distressed and nondistressed married couples. J Consult Clin Psychol 47:368–376, 1979

Brown GW, Harris T: Social Origins of Depression: A Study of Psychiatric Disorder in Women. London, Tavistock, 1978

Brown GW, Birley JLT, Wing JK: Influence of family life on the course of schizophrenic disorders: a replication. Br J Psychiatry 121:241–258, 1972

Bullock RC, Siegel R, Weissman MM, et al: The weeping wife: marital relations of depressed women. Journal of Marriage and the Family 34:488–495, 1972

Coleman RE, Miller AG: The relation between depression and marital maladjustment in a clinic population: a multitrait-multimethod study. J Consult Clin Psychol 43:647–651, 1975

Crowther JH: The relationship between depression and marital maladjustment: a descriptive study. J Nerv Ment Dis 173:227–231, 1985

Falloon IRH, Boyd JI, McGill CW, et al: Family management in the prevention of exacerbations of schizophrenia. N Engl J Med 306:1437–1440, 1982

Falloon IRH, Boyd JL, McGill CW: Family Care of Schizophrenia. New York, Guilford Press, 1984

Gotlib I, Hooley JM: Depression and marital distress: current status and future directions, in Handbook of Personal Relationships. Edited by Duck S. New York, Wiley, 1988

Gottman JM: Marital Interaction: Experimental Investigations. New York, Academic Press, 1979

Gottman JM, Markman HJ, Notarius C: The topography of marital conflict: a sequential analysis of verbal and nonverbal behavior. Journal of Marriage and the Family 39:461–477, 1977

Hahlweg K, Goldstein MJ: Understanding Major Mental Disorder: The Contribution of Family Interaction Research. New York, Family Process Press, 1987

Hahlweg K, Reisner L, Kohli G, et al: Development and validity of a new system to analyze interpersonal communication (KPI: Kategoriensystem für Partnerschaftlische Interaktion), in Marital Interaction: Analysis and Modification. Edited by Hahlweg K, Jacobson NS. New York, Academic Press, 1984a, pp 182–198

Hahlweg K, Revenstorf D, Schindler L: Effects of behavioral marital therapy on couples' communication and problem-solving skills. J Consult Clin Psychol 52:553–566, 1984b

Henderson S: Social relationships, adversity and neurosis: an analysis of prospective observations. Br J Psychiatry 138:391–398, 1981

Hinchliffe MK, Hooper D, Roberts FJ: The Melancholy Marriage. New York, Wiley, 1978

Hogarty GE, Anderson CM, Reiss DJ, et al: Family psychoeducation, social skills training, and maintenance chemotherapy in the aftercare treatment of schizophrenia. Arch Gen Psychiatry 43:633–642, 1986

Hooley JM: Expressed emotion: a review of the critical literature. Clinical Psychology Review 5:119–139, 1985

Hooley JM: Expressed emotion and depression: interactions between patients and high- versus low-EE spouses. J Abnorm Psychol 95:237–246, 1986

Hooley JM, Hahlweg K: The marriages and interaction patterns of depressed patients and their spouses: comparison of high and low EE dyads, in Treatment of Schizophrenia: Family Assessment and Intervention. Edited by Goldstein MJ, Hand I, Hahlweg K. Berlin, Springer-Verlag, 1986

Hooley JM, Teasdale JD: Predictors of relapse in unipolar depressives: expressed emotion, marital distress and perceived criticism. J Abnorm Psychol (in press)

Hooley JM, Orley J, Teasdale JD: Levels of expressed emotion and relapse in depressed patients. Br J Psychiatry 148:642–647, 1986

Jenkins JH, Karno M, de la Selva A, et al: Expressed emotion, maintenance psychotherapy, and schizophrenic relapse among Mexican-Americans. Psychopharmacol Bull 22:621–627, 1986

Karno M, Jenkins JH, de la Selva A, et al: Expressed emotion and schizophrenic outcome among Mexican-American families. J Nerv Ment Dis 175:143–151, 1987

Koren P, Carlton K, Shaw D: Marital conflict: relation among behaviors, outcomes, and distress. J Consult Clin Psychol 48:460–468, 1980

Leff JP, Kuipers L, Berkowitz R, et al: A controlled trial of social intervention in the families of schizophrenic patients. Br J Psychiatry 141:121–134, 1982

Leff J, Wig NN, Bedi H, et al: Influences of relatives' expressed emotion on the course of schizophrenia in Chandigarh. Br J Psychiatry 151:166–173, 1987

Miklowitz DJ, Goldstein MJ, Falloon IRH: Premorbid and symptomatic characteristics of patients from families with high and low levels of expressed emotion. J Abnorm Psychol 92:359–367, 1983

Miklowitz DJ, Goldstein MJ, Nuechterlein KH, et al: The family and the course of recent onset mania, in Understanding Major Mental Disorder: The Contribution of Family Interaction Research. Edited by Hahlweg K, Goldstein MJ. New York, Family Process Press, 1987

Paykel ES, Myers JK, Dienelt MN, et al: Life events and depression: a controlled study. Arch Gen Psychiatry 21:753–760, 1969

Paykel ES, Emms EM, Fletcher J, et al: Life events and social support in puerperal depression. Br J Psychiatry 136:339–346, 1980

Revenstorf D, Vogel B, Wegener C, et al: Escalation phenomena in interaction sequences. Behavior Analysis and Modification 2:97–116, 1980

Revenstorf D, Hahlweg K, Schindler L, et al: Interaction analysis of marital conflict, in Marital Interaction: Analysis and Modification. Edited by Hahlweg K, Jacobson NS. New York, Guilford Press, 1984

Sackett GP: The lag sequential analysis of contingency and cyclicity in behavioral interaction research, in Handbook of Infant Development. Edited by Osofsky J. New York, Wiley, 1977

Spanier G: Measuring dyadic adjustment: new scales for assessing the quality of marriage and similar dyads. Journal of Marriage and the Family 38:15–28, 1976

Spitzer RL, Endicott J, Robins E: Research Diagnostic Criteria (RDC) for a Select Group of Functional Disorders. New York, Biometrics Research, 1978

Strodtbeck FL: Husband-wife interaction over revealed differences. American Sociological Review 16:468–473, 1951

Vaughn CE: Patterns of emotional response in the families of schizophrenic patients, in Treatment of Schizophrenia: Family Assessment and Intervention. Edited by Goldstein MJ, Hand I, Hahlweg K. Berlin, Springer-Verlag, 1986

Vaughn CE, Leff JP: The influence of family and social factors on the course of psychiatric illness: a comparison of schizophrenic and depressed neurotic patients. Br J Psychiatry 129:125–137, 1976a

Vaughn CE, Leff JP: The measurement of expressed emotion in the families of psychiatric patients. Br J Soc Psychol 15:157–165, 1976b

Vaughn CE, Snyder KS, Freeman W, et al: Family factors in schizophrenic relapse. Arch Gen Psychiatry 41:1169–1177, 1984

Weissman MM, Paykel ES: The Depressed Woman: A Study of Social Relationships. Chicago, IL, University of Chicago Press, 1974

Wing JK, Cooper JE, Sartorius N: The Description of Psychiatric Symptoms: An Introduction Manual for the PSE and Catego System. London, Cambridge University Press, 1974

Chapter 4

Psychopathology in Offspring of Parents With Affective Disorders

Kathleen R. Merikangas, Ph.D.
Myrna M. Weissman, Ph.D.
Brigitte A. Prusoff, Ph.D.

Chapter 4

Psychopathology in Offspring of Parents With Affective Disorders

Familial aggregation has been frequently observed among probands with depression, anxiety disorders, and alcoholism (Gershon et al. 1976; Goodwin 1983; Crowe et al. 1983). Because of the familial nature of these disorders, offspring of such probands have been identified to be at high risk for developing these illnesses themselves (Tarter 1983). Information regarding this risk has come from several sources: retrospective studies of patients with psychiatric disorders, studies of children whose parents are being treated for these disorders, and longitudinal follow-up studies of children with symptoms of the disorders.

Although most studies of high-risk children have been conducted with children of schizophrenic mothers, there is increasing evidence that children of parents with depression, alcoholism, and anxiety disorders are also at increased risk for psychopathology. Reviews of the literature have shown high rates of symptomatology and impairment in offspring of probands with major depression (Orvaschel et al. 1980; McKnew et al. 1979; Beardslee et al. 1983), with a prevalence of diagnosable illness in the offspring ranging from 33 to 45%, most of it affective in nature. A family history of depression appears to be the major risk factor for depression in children. Negative environmental factors such as family discord, instability, and disruption are consistently reported in retrospective studies of depressed adults and in studies of children with depression (Orvaschel et al. 1980).

This research was supported in part by Alcohol, Drug Abuse, and Mental Health Administration Grants MH-28274 and AA-07080, National Institute of Mental Health, Rockville, Maryland; by the Yale Mental Health Clinical Research Center, MH-30929; and by the Research Scientist Development Award, MH-00499 (K.R.M.).

Children of alcoholic parents have an even greater risk of suffering from the numerous disorders than has been reported for children with depressed parents. Infants born to mothers who drink heavily during pregnancy may develop fetal alcohol syndrome, which is characterized by physical, emotional, and intellectual deficits (Steinhausen et al. 1982). Children of alcoholic parents have an approximately fourfold greater risk of developing alcoholism than children of nonalcoholic parents, with males at a much greater risk than females; the effects of paternal versus maternal alcoholism may differ as well (Cloninger et al. 1979). The unstable home environment in which these children are raised has likewise been well documented as characterized by family disruption, frequent divorce, and low socioeconomic status (Adler and Raphael 1983). An association between childhood conduct disorder and adult alcoholism has been demonstrated in retrospective studies of alcoholic persons and prospective studies of children with hyperactivity and conduct problems (Goodwin et al. 1975; Cadoret and Gath 1978; Alterman et al. 1982).

Although the risk of psychopathology in offspring of parents with anxiety disorders has not been established, studies of the relatives of adults with panic disorder, phobia, obsessive-compulsive disorder, and generalized anxiety disorder show an increased risk of anxiety disorder compared with normal populations (Crowe et al. 1983). However, the lack of specificity of transmission is notable for most of the disorders, with the exception of panic disorder and possibly obsessive-compulsive disorder. The diagnostic overlap both within the anxiety disorders and between anxiety disorders and affective disorders presents a major difficulty in interpreting family studies in this area. Weissman et al. (1984) found that children under the age of 18 of parents with depression and either agoraphobia or panic disorder had an increased risk of separation anxiety, panic disorder, and phobic disorders compared with children of parents with major depression only or normal controls. This finding has been confirmed in a more recent direct interview study of these children (Weissman et al. 1987a, 1987b).

Several studies have reported a link between childhood school refusal or separation anxiety and either phobic anxiety or panic disorder in adulthood (Berg et al. 1974; Gittelman-Klein 1975). In general, studies of the early history of agoraphobic adults report the onset of phobias before age 10 in a large proportion (Sheehan et al. 1981).

Although there is a consensus in the above studies that offspring of probands with the above-cited psychiatric disorders are at increased risk for psychopathology, there are few data regarding the mechanism for the elevated risk. Twin and cross-fostering studies have established the involvement of genetic factors in at least some subtypes of these disorders. Also, the negative home environments of these children are noted throughout, and all of the major psychiatric disorders are related to major and chronic disruption in the parental role. Bothwell and Weissman (1977) reported that social role impairment of depressed women persisted up to 4 years after cessation of the acute episode of depression. Impaired marital functioning of both depressed and alcoholic patients has been a consistent finding. Thus, it is likely that genetic predisposition is potentiated by the detrimental environment that is so often characteristic of parents with these disorders.

One phenomenon related to both familial disruption and elevated risk to offspring is concordance for psychiatric disorders in parents. The present study therefore focused on the effects of parental concordance for psychiatric illness in general and affective illness in particular.

Previous reports from our family study of 215 probands and their 456 offspring over the age of 6 have shown that when parents are concordant for alcoholism, children are more likely to become alcoholic themselves and are also more likely to develop conduct disorder in childhood and antisocial personality in adulthood (Merikangas et al. 1985). Similar findings emerged for depression and anxiety disorders. There was a linear relationship between the number of ill parents and rates of depression and/or anxiety disorders in children (Weissman et al. 1984). However, these data were considered preliminary because the children had not been interviewed directly.

METHODS

Probands

The analysis reported herein is based on 133 white probands with major depression defined according to modified Research Diagnostic Criteria (RDC), who were in treatment at the Yale University Depression Research Unit or other facilities in the Department of Psychiatry. They were group matched by sex and age with 82 normal controls who had no history of psychiatric illness and who were obtained from the 1975 community survey by Weissman and Myers (1978). Complete pedigrees for each proband were systematically obtained, and diagnostic assessments according to RDC were made for every (living or dead) adult first-degree relative and spouse.

The depressed probands were classified according to the presence or absence of other diagnoses, such as alcoholism and anxiety disorders. The onset of alcoholism in all of the probands was chronologically secondary to major depression. All probands with primary alcoholism or antisocial personality were excluded from the study. Anxiety disorder included agoraphobia, panic disorder, or generalized anxiety disorder and could have occurred either concomitant with or temporally separate from depressive episodes.

Direct interviews were obtained from adult relatives and spouses whenever possible. If not, family history data were obtained from multiple informants and from medical records. Direct interviews were conducted with 40% of the sample, and family history information was available from multiple informants in over 55% of the relatives. Diagnostic assessments of the relatives were made blindly with respect to status of the proband, using a best-estimate procedure (Leckman et al. 1982). Diagnoses of adult relatives and spouses were made according to modified RDC and were based on all available information.

At the time of the original study, offspring under age 18 were not directly interviewed, because diagnostic instruments and procedures for the assessment of psychiatric disorders in children were not available. A direct interview study of children was initiated 6 years after the original study had begun. All probands with offspring under age 18 at the time of the original proband interview were recruited for participation in the high-risk study. Eighty-seven percent of the eligible probands agreed to participate.

To determine the current clinical status and social functioning of the parents, each parent was interviewed separately by independent interviewers. A third interviewer interviewed a parent (preferably the mother) about the child and, at another time, interviewed the child about himself or herself, in order to obtain a comprehensive assessment of the child's psychiatric, behavioral, and social functioning. Parents were asked to complete self-administered reports about themselves and about each of their children, and children (approximately 10 years and over) were asked to complete self-administered reports about themselves. Authorized by both parent and child, we asked each child's teacher, pediatrician, and, when indicated, other health-care providers to complete questionnaires about the child. Direct interviews were obtained with 83% of the eligible children, and 97% of the children had a report from at least one parent. Eighty-four percent of the mothers and 72% of the fathers also completed the diagnostic interviews about themselves.

The interviewers had a minimum of 5 years of clinical experience with children and included two child psychologists, two child psychiatry fellows, and two masters-level school psychologists. They were blind to the diagnostic status of the parent for the child interviews and blind to the clinical status of both the child and the previous data on parents for the interviews on current parent status.

Assessment of Children

Adapted for use in longitudinal studies as a reliable and valid instrument for obtaining lifetime diagnoses, the Kiddie-SADS-E (Puig-Antich 1982; Orvaschel et al. 1982; Chambers et al. 1985) and the DSM-III addenda were used in our pilot study at the Yale Psychiatric Institute to assess diagnoses in the children. Findings suggest that interviewing a parent and child separately and combining the results of the two interviews provide a more complete and accurate diagnostic assessment of the child. The Kiddie-SADS-E is the core of a comprehensive interview that we assembled to be administered to a parent about the child and to the child about himself or herself. A more detailed description of the assessment procedures of the children is given by Weissman et al. (1987a, 1987b).

Best-Estimate Diagnoses

A best-estimate diagnostic procedure was used in which a child psychiatrist and clinical psychologist who were not involved in the interviewing reviewed all sources of information and independently assigned a diagnosis. Discrepancies were resolved by a third source, who also independently and blindly reviewed all available information. We plan to reinterview all offspring and parents in 2 years. The initial level of agreement was 83%.

RESULTS

There were 215 probands in the original study, of whom 165 had offspring. Of these, 239 adult offspring were assessed in the original study with the SADS-L and Family History RDC, and 220 offspring ages 6–23 were assessed in the high-risk component of the study with the Kiddie-SADS-E, for a total of 459 offspring for whom diagnostic assessments were completed.

The age and sex distributions of the offspring are shown in Table 1. There were approximately equal numbers of male and female offspring, and most of the offspring were between the ages of 18 and 24. A substantial proportion of the offspring were well into adulthood. The number of children per family did not differ between the two proband groups.

The lifetime prevalence rates of disorders among the offspring according to the original proband group of their parent are shown in Table 2. There was a twofold increase in the rates of major depression among the offspring of depressed probands compared with normal probands. Major depression in the offspring was defined according to modified RDC as in our adult sample: four major symptoms; 4 weeks duration; and impairment. Anxiety disorders were also significantly more prevalent among offspring of the depressed probands. Rates of alcoholism and conduct disorder or antisocial personality were not significantly higher among the offspring of the depressed compared with the normal probands.

Because a large proportion of the spouses of both the depressed and normal probands also had psychiatric diagnoses and because of the large number of secondary diagnoses in the probands, disorders in the offspring were also examined according to the diagnoses of both parents, rather than by the original case-control design. Thus, normal control probands with spouses with psychiatric illness were reclassified by the diagnosis of their spouses. Table 3 shows the number of parents ill by diagnosis; these diagnostic groupings are

Table 1. Number of offspring by age and sex

	Age	Male	Female	Total
High-risk study	<12	20	15	35
	12–17	39	53	92
	18–24	46	47	93
Family study	18–24	58	52	110
	≥25	65	64	129
Total		228	231	459

Table 2. Proportion of offspring with diagnoses by proband group

	Diagnosis in proband parent	
Diagnosis in offspring	Depressed (n = 273)	Normal (n = 186)
Major depression	23.4*	11.3
Alcoholism	7.7	8.6
Conduct disorder/antisocial personality	15.8	10.7
Anxiety disorder	34.8*	22.6
Any psychiatric diagnosis	67.8*	52.2

Note. Values are percentages.
*$P < .01$.

not mutually exclusive. That is, in all of the couples in which both members were affected, at least one parent had major depression. From Table 3, it can be seen that concordance for major depression, anxiety disorders, and any psychiatric diagnosis was fairly common, whereas concordance for alcoholism was not. This may be attributed to the sampling of probands with major depression, in which primary alcoholism was an exclusion criterion.

Table 4 presents the rates of major depression and any RDC diagnosis among the first-degree relatives of the spouses of the depressed probands. This analysis shows that the relatives of the spouses with major depression had significantly higher rates of major depression and any RDC diagnosis than the relatives of the spouses who did not have major depression. Similarly, the relatives of the spouses with any RDC diagnosis also had a significantly increased risk of

Table 3. Parental mating types by diagnosis

	Parental mating type (%)		
Diagnosis in parent	Both	One	Neither
Major depression	15.7	50.9	33.3
Alcoholism	4.8	14.5	80.6
Anxiety disorder	10.3	44.2	45.5
Any psychiatric diagnosis	41.2	38.2	20.6

Note. n = 165 couples.

Table 4. Lifetime prevalence of psychiatric disorders among parents and siblings of spouses of probands with major depression

	Lifetime prevalence among first-degree relatives of spouse (%)	
Diagnosis in spouse	Major depression	Any RDC diagnosis
Major depression		
Present	4.8	25.5
Absent	1.4*	16.7*
Any RDC diagnosis		
Present	3.0	23.4**
Absent	1.3	12.5

Note. RDC = Research Diagnostic Criteria.
$^{*}P < .05$. $^{**}P < .001$.

any RDC diagnosis compared with the relatives of the spouses who did not meet RDC for any lifetime diagnosis. This suggests that there was familial aggregation of major depression and psychiatric illness in general in the families of the spouses who had major depression and those with any RDC diagnosis. From these results, one can conclude that it is likely that the concordance for major depression between the probands and their spouses can be attributed to assortative mating for depression or some related trait rather than to marital interaction resulting in the occurrence of depression in the spouse of the depressed proband.

Table 5 shows the relationship between any psychiatric illness in parents and disorders in offspring. The strongest linear trend was observed for any psychiatric diagnosis in offspring. That is, when neither parent was affected, one-third of the children had a diagnosis; when one parent was ill, over one-half of the children had a diagnosis; and when both parents were affected, three-quarters of their offspring had a diagnosable psychiatric illness.

Major depression, anxiety disorders, and antisocial personality/conduct disorder also showed significant linear trends according to the number of parents with any RDC diagnosis. Alcoholism was the only diagnostic category among children that was not related to parental concordance for any psychiatric diagnosis.

Table 6 shows the effects of parental concordance for alcoholism. There is a strong linear trend in the relationship of rates of alcohol dependence among offspring and the number of parents with al-

Table 5. Proportion of offspring with diagnoses by parental mating type for any psychiatric disorder

	Parental mating type for any psychiatric disorder			
Diagnosis in offspring	Both (n = 201)	One (n = 173)	Neither (n = 85)	χ^{2a}
Major depression	29.4	23.7	14.1	7.38*
Alcoholism	8.0	8.1	8.2	0.01
Conduct disorder/antisocial personality	17.4	14.5	3.5	8.51*
Anxiety disorder	41.8	23.7	14.1	25.99**
Any psychiatric diagnosis	75.1	57.8	36.5	39.05**

Note. Values are percentages.
[a]Linear trend in proportions, 1 df.
*$P < .01$. **$P < .001$.

coholism. Offspring with one alcoholic parent had a twofold increase in rates of alcoholism compared with offspring of parents without alcoholism. Likewise, offspring of couples concordant for alcoholism had a threefold increase in rates of alcoholism compared with those in which one parent was affected. Similarly for antisocial personality and conduct disorder, there was a strong significant linear trend according to the number of parents with alcoholism. Rates of major depression and anxiety disorders were not significantly increased among offspring of alcoholic parents.

The effects of parental concordance for alcoholism and any RDC diagnosis on the lifetime prevalence rates of diagnoses in offspring are summarized in Table 7. Alcoholism is the disorder for which parental assortative mating was associated with the greatest increase in the rate of the same disorder among offspring. Offspring with two alcoholic parents had a threefold increase in rates of alcoholism compared with offspring of couples in which only one parent had alcoholism. Nearly 50% of the offspring over age 18 of the couples concordant for alcoholism had alcoholism themselves, compared to 11% when neither parent had alcoholism. The effect of assortative mating for alcoholism was also seen in the increased risk of antisocial personality in the offspring over age 18: 30% had antisocial personality compared to 2% of the offspring of couples without alcoholism. There was a 1.7-fold increase in the risk of conduct disorder in the younger offspring and of antisocial personality in the older offspring of parents who were concordant for alcoholism.

Table 6. Proportion of offspring with diagnoses by parental mating type for alcoholism

	Parental mating type for alcoholism			
Diagnosis in offspring	Both (n = 25)	One (n = 84)	Neither (n = 350)	χ^{2a}
Major depression	28.0	17.9	18.0	.80
Alcoholism	32.0	10.7	5.7	18.77**
Conduct disorder/antisocial personality	36.0	21.4	10.3	18.07**
Anxiety disorder	44.0	32.1	28.3	2.67
Any psychiatric diagnosis	80.0	69.1	58.3	7.16*

Note. Values are percentages.
[a]Linear trend in proportions, 1 df.
*$P < .05$. **$P < .01$.

Table 7. Summary of effects of parental concordance for alcoholism on diagnoses in offspring

Concordance in parents	Diagnosis with increased prevalence in offspring	Relative risk (both vs. one parent with diagnosis)
Alcoholism	Alcoholism	3.0
	Conduct disorder (offspring ≤ age 18) or Antisocial personality (offspring > age 18)	1.7
Any diagnosis	Anxiety disorders	1.8
	Any diagnosis	1.3

Note. $N = 456$.

Last, parental concordance for any RDC diagnosis was related to extremely high rates of diagnoses in offspring, with an average of 70–80% being affected. Concordance for any RDC diagnosis in parents was related to a 1.8-fold increase in the rates of anxiety disorders and a 1.3-fold increase in the rates of any diagnosis in offspring compared with those in offspring with one parent ill.

DISCUSSION

The results indicate that parental concordance for psychiatric illness in general and alcoholism in particular is related to an increased risk of psychiatric disorders in the offspring. The findings from our earlier studies in which the information on children was derived from family history, rather than direct interviews, were confirmed in these analyses. The effects of parental concordance for major depression and anxiety disorders have been presented elsewhere (Merikangas et al. 1988).

Also consistent with earlier studies was a high degree of concordance for psychiatric illness among the parents, with 41% of the couples consisting of dual matings for psychiatric disorders (Merikangas 1982). Concordance between spouses for a disorder does not necessarily imply that assortative mating for that trait occurred. Such concordance could result from convergence for the trait as a result of marital interaction. However, evidence regarding aggregation of the trait among first-degree relatives of the spouse with the trait, who do not share the environment with the proband, would exclude the latter explanation. From our data, it was concluded that assortative mating had occurred because increased rates of psychopathology were observed among the relatives of the ill spouses compared with those of the well spouses.

Concordance for a trait does not imply that mating has occurred for that particular trait. Rather, mate selection may involve another factor that may be a correlate or precursor to the trait for which concordance is assessed. Indeed, differential mate selection among persons with affective disorders is unlikely because the onset of these disorders in both spouses generally occurs several years after the time of marriage. We have previously suggested that mate selection in these couples may be related to personality factors that are premorbid to affective disorders or to similar levels of social differentiation (Merikangas and Spiker 1982).

These data clearly demonstrate that offspring of concordant parents are at significantly increased risk of developing psychopathology. We have also demonstrated some degree of specificity of transmission of the effects of assortative mating as well, with children exhibiting a tendency to develop the same disorders as those that are manifest in their parents. Such specificity may be attributable to shared liability, modeling of parental behavior, or a combination thereof.

Evidence for continuity between childhood and adulthood manifestation of similar syndromes was provided by the remarkably similar increase in the relative risks of disorders among the younger and older offspring of couples in particular mating classes. For example, similar elevations of risk were observed for conduct disorder among younger offspring and antisocial personality among adult offspring of dual-mated alcoholic couples compared with those of other parental mating types. In contrast, little continuity was observed between conduct disorder and antisocial personality among the younger and older offspring of parental mating for depression alone.

Although assortative mating among parents has been shown to be an important risk factor for the development of psychopathology in their children, the mechanism by which this increased risk occurs is not known. It is likely that assortative mating is related to both increased genetic risk and a clustering of environmental risk factors. Couples with concordance for affective disorders have been found to have significantly greater impairment in marital and social adjustment and an elevated divorce rate compared with couples in which only one member is affected (Merikangas et al. 1983; Merikangas 1984).

These data clearly demonstrate that offspring of parents concordant for psychiatric disorders are at significantly increased risk of developing psychopathology. The implications of these findings in terms of primary prevention, the ultimate aim of high-risk studies, are not clear. Genetic counseling of prospective couples in which both have a family history of depression, anxiety disorders, or alcoholism is an unlikely intervention. However, efforts toward secondary intervention depend on the identification of the specific factors that comprise appropriate targets of prevention and intervention. Our study and those of others have identified the presence of parental concordance for depression, alcoholism, and other disorders as one such factor related to significantly increased risk in children. Efforts at identification of such situations by routine assessment of the spouse of patients who come for treatment and application of interventions that attempt to minimize the marital and parental role impairment may help to decrease the substantially elevated rates of psychiatric disorders in the children examined in this study.

REFERENCES

Adler R, Raphael B: Review: children of alcoholics. Aust N Z J Psychiatry 17:3–8, 1983

Alterman AA, Petraulo E, Tarter R: Hyperactivity and alcoholism: familial and behavioral correlates. Addict Behav 7:413–421, 1982

American Psychiatric Association: Diagnostic and Statistical Manual of Mental Disorders, 3rd Edition. Washington, DC, American Psychiatric Association, 1980

Beardslee WR, Bemporad J, Keller MB, et al: Children of parents with major affective disorders: a review. Am J Psychiatry 140:825–832, 1983

Berg I, Marks I, McGuire R, et al: School phobia and agoraphobics. Psychol Med 4:428–434, 1974

Bothwell S, Weissman MM: Social impairments four years after an acute depressive episode. Am J Orthopsychiatry 47:231–237, 1977

Cadoret RJ, Gath A: Inheritance of alcoholism in adoptees. Br J Psychiatry 132:252–258, 1978

Chambers W, Puig-Antich J, Hirsch M, et al: The assessment of affective disorders in children and adolescents by semi-structured interview. Arch Gen Psychiatry 42:696–702, 1985

Cloninger CR, Reich T, Wetzel R: Alcoholism and affective disorders: familial associations and genetic models, in Alcoholism and Affective Disorders: Clinical, Genetic and Biochemical Studies. Edited by Goodwin DW, Erickson CK. New York, SP Medical and Scientific, 1979, pp 57–86

Crowe RR, Noyes R, Pauls DL, et al: A family study of panic disorder. Arch Gen Psychiatry 40:1065–1069, 1983

Gershon ES, Bunney WE Jr, Leckman JF, et al: The inheritance of affective disorders: a review of data and hypotheses. Behav Genet 6:227–261, 1976

Gittelman-Klein R: Psychiatric characteristics of the relatives of school phobic children, in Mental Health in Children. Edited by Siva Sankar DV. New York, PJD, 1975

Goodwin DW: Alcoholism, in The Child at Psychiatric Risk. Edited by Tarter RE. New York, Oxford University Press, 1983, pp 195–213

Goodwin DW, Schulsinger F, Hermansen L, et al: Alcoholism and the hyperactive child syndrome. J Nerv Ment Dis 160:349–353, 1975

Leckman JF, Sholomskas D, Thompson WD, et al: Best estimate of lifetime psychiatric diagnosis. Arch Gen Psychiatry 39:879–883, 1982

McKnew DH, Cytryn L, Efron AM, et al: Offspring of patients with affective disorders. Br J Psychiatry 134:148–152, 1979

Merikangas KR: Assortative mating for psychiatric disorders and psychological traits. Arch Gen Psychiatry 39:1173–1180, 1982

Merikangas KR: Divorce and assortative mating among depressed patients. Am J Psychiatry 141:74–76, 1984

Merikangas KR, Spiker DG: Assortative mating among inpatients with primary affective disorder. Psychol Med 12:753–764, 1982

Merikangas KR, Bromet EJ, Spiker DJ: Assortative mating, social adjustment, and course of illness in primary affective disorder. Arch Gen Psychiatry 40:795–800, 1983

Merikangas KR, Weissman MM, Prusoff BA, et al: Depressives with secondary alcoholism: psychiatric disorders in offspring. J Stud Alcohol 46:199–204, 1985

Merikangas KR, Prusoff BA, Weissman MM: Parental concordance for affective disorders: psychopathology in offspring. J Affective Disord 15:279–290, 1988

Orvaschel H, Weissman MM, Kidd KK: Children and depression: the children of depressed parents, the childhood of depressed patients; depression in children. J Affective Disord 2:1–16, 1980

Orvaschel H, Puig-Antich J, Chambers W, et al: Retrospective assessments of prepubertal major depression with the Kiddie-SADS-E. J Am Acad Child Psychiatry 21:392–397, 1982

Puig-Antich J: The use of the RDC criteria for major depressive disorder in children and adolescents. J Am Acad Child Psychiatry 21:291–293, 1982

Sheehan DV, Sheehan KE, Minichiello WE: Age of onset of phobic disorders: a reevaluation. Compr Psychiatry 22:544–553, 1981

Steinhausen HC, Nestler V, Spohr HL: Development of psychopathology of children with the fetal alcohol syndrome. J Dev Behav Pediatr 3:49–54, 1982

Tarter R (ed): The Child at Psychiatric Risk. New York, Oxford University Press, 1983

Weissman MM, Myers JK: Affective disorders in a US urban community. Arch Gen Psychiatry 35:1304–1311, 1978

Weissman MM, Leckman JF, Merikangas KR, et al: Depression and anxiety disorders in the children (ages 6–17) of parents with depression and anxiety disorders. Arch Gen Psychiatry 41:845–852, 1984

Weissman MM, Wickramaratne P, Warner V, et al: Assessing psychiatric disorders in children: discrepancies between mothers' and children's reports. Arch Gen Psychiatry 44:747–753, 1987a

Weissman MM, Gammon GD, John K, et al: Children of depressed parents: increased psychopathology and early onset of major depression. Arch Gen Psychiatry 44:847–853, 1987b

Chapter 5

Development of a Preventive Intervention for Families in Which Parents Have Serious Affective Disorder

William R. Beardslee, M.D.

Chapter 5

Development of a Preventive Intervention for Families in Which Parents Have Serious Affective Disorder

Youngsters who grow up in families in which parents have serious affective disorder are more likely to develop psychopathology and social impairment over the course of adolescence than comparison groups (Welner et al. 1977; Cytryn et al. 1982; Weissman et al. 1984a; Beardslee et al. 1985a; Welner and Garrison 1985; Waters 1987). Investigators have emphasized the need for preventive intervention programs for such youngsters (Philips 1983; Grunebaum 1984). Surprisingly, given the high rates of affective disorder in the general population (Weissman and Myers 1987) and the large number of clinicians of various disciplines who treat affective disorders in adults, programs focused on preventive intervention for children and adolescents in these families have not yet appeared.

Advances in both conceptualization and design have made possible some sound empirical studies of successful psychosocial preventive interventions in other areas, including early interventions with high-risk youngsters such as Head Start and related endeavors (Zigler and Valentine 1979; McKey et al. 1985; Lazar and Darlington 1982; Berrueta-Clement et al. 1985) and numerous school-based interventions (Kolvin et al. 1981; Chandler et al. 1985).

Within the area of the primary prevention of depression, empirical efforts have focused mainly on adults (Munoz 1987) and have ex-

This work was supported by a Faculty Scholar Award of the William T. Grant Foundation to Dr. Beardslee and by the Overseas Shipholding Group, Inc., and the Harris Trust through Harvard Medical School.

plored cognitive behavioral approaches because of the success of cognitive therapies in the treatment of depressed adults (Lewinsohn 1987; Rush 1987). Field trials of cognitive behavioral strategies are now under way in the prevention of depression in adults recruited from general medical clinics (Munoz et al. 1987) and Hispanic women in difficult economic and social situations (Vega et al. 1987). Programs for adolescents already reporting some symptoms and those at high risk for depression in school-based samples because of low self-esteem or other factors have been proposed, but have not yet been implemented or evaluated (Rehm 1987; Ginsburg and Twentyman 1987).

In terms of secondary and tertiary prevention, the studies by Falloon et al. (1987) have clearly demonstrated that family-based interventions after an episode of schizophrenia in a family member do substantially increase that individual's functioning and social adjustment and contribute to the prevention of relapse.

In the history of the mental hygiene movement, claims have often far outstripped what could be accomplished through prevention (Spaulding and Balch 1983). Although an increasing sophistication has characterized both the dialogue and the research conducted in preventive intervention in recent years (Munoz 1987; Rolf 1985; Chassin et al. 1985; Earls 1987; Eisenberg 1981), there are substantial methodological problems in demonstrating preventive effects (Rutter 1982; Eisenberg 1984).

Investigators have agreed that prevention programs must have specified interventions with clearly targeted goals and measurable outcomes in order to constitute reasonable empirical approaches to the problem. Two separate approaches have merit. One is based on disease prevention by the identification of a specific etiological agent and the removal of that agent, whether of genetic, infectious, metabolic, or psychosocial origin. The second is based on encouraging or developing the inherent adaptive capacities of individuals (such as Head Start).

Within the literature, there are no family-based preventive interventions to be used by clinicians in dealing with families in which parents have had serious affective disorders. It is the purpose of this report to describe the development of such an intervention with specific focus on what is amenable to efforts by clinicians in a short-term format. It is designed to be used by interveners from a variety of disciplines—internists, pediatricians, social workers, psychiatrists, and psychologists. Given the lack of previous studies, a detailed review of the empirical evidence about the nature of risk and resiliency in the children of parents with affective disorder is presented. Based on this review, a preventive intervention strategy for use by clinicians is described, and pilot experience that draws on clinical work with families is presented.

EMPIRICAL FINDINGS—CHILDREN OF PARENTS WITH AFFECTIVE DISORDER

Psychopathology

Five separate recent empirical investigations concur in demonstrating higher lifetime rates of diagnosable general psychopathology and higher rates of episodes of major depression in the offspring (ages 6–19) of parents who presented for psychiatric treatment for affective disorder compared with children in families without illness. These studies used standard structured research interviews scored according to criterion-based diagnostic systems (Cytryn et al. 1982; Weissman et al. 1984a; Beardslee et al. 1985a; Welner and Garrison 1985). Lower overall rates of adaptive functioning in children of parents with affective disorder were also described in several of these studies. These findings are supported by a large number of other investigations that used various methodologies (Waters 1987; Zuckerman and Beardslee 1987). Adolescence is a time of heightened risk. The incidence of episodes of major depression in the children of parents with affective disorders increases significantly throughout adolescence. The occurrence of an episode of affective disorder by the end of adolescence in youngsters at risk ranges between 10 and 40% in the four studies using structured interviews mentioned above.

Examination of nine cases of major depression from one of these risk studies (Beardslee et al. 1985b) has shown that these disorders cause major disruptions in the youngsters' lives. The children were studied because their parents had affective disorder, not because they presented for treatment. Seven children had episodes lasting 6 weeks or more, and four children experienced more than one episode. The shortest episode lasted for 4 weeks. Three of the nine children had suicidal thoughts that were expressed to a parent or others. All reported persistent feelings of worthlessness, guilt, and self-reproach. All reported periods of social withdrawal. The severity of social impairment ranged from the loss of interest in usual activities to pervasive withdrawn behavior and refusal to get out of bed. In all children, symptoms of the disorder lasted longer than the period during which the episode met full criteria. All the children experienced difficulties in school. Two-thirds of these adolescent depressions were unrecognized and untreated, sometimes even for years. This emphasizes the need to alert families about what youngsters are likely to experience and assist them in getting help as early as possible in the course of the illness.

Retrospective assessments have demonstrated a variable pattern for the timing of adolescent disorder in relation to parental disorder; i.e., some youngsters become ill shortly after parental illness, and others somewhat later, often at the time of the onset of puberty or other related stressors. Some youngsters exhibit a diagnosable disorder, whereas others only display limitations in their relationships or school performance (Beardslee et al. 1987). Thus, an intervention program must be flexible because the nature, course, and timing of the youngsters' difficulties will vary.

Studies of the parental predictors of child disorder (in addition to an affective diagnosis) have shown that lowered social status, poor marital functioning, and increased severity and chronicity of affective disorder are all correlated with poorer outcomes in youngsters (Keller et al. 1986). The presence of several diagnoses in parents rather than just affective disorder often leads to poorer outcome in youngsters (Weissman et al. 1984b). There has been increased awareness of the chronic nature of affective illness in adults, particularly the combination of a chronic depression along with acute episodes (Keller et al. 1983), as has there been with children (Kovacs et al. 1984; Keller et al., in press). Only about a third of adults with depression receive adequate treatment (Keller et al. 1982). Numerous authors have drawn attention to the fact that often both parents are impaired in families with affective illness, either through assortative mating or other mechanisms (Merikangas 1984). This has particularly severe consequences for youngsters (Beardslee et al. 1985a; Weissman et al. 1984b). Taken together, these data emphasize the need for ongoing treatment of affective disorder in adults. Clinicians must also be alert to factors in addition to the presence of affective disorder in parents, such as illness in the spouse and marital discord.

One aspect of research on children at risk for affective disorder has particular relevance to prevention. Each of the previously described reports of poor outcome with parental affective disorder compared children from families in which a parent not only had an affective disorder but was selected for study when the parent sought treatment (the clinical sample) with children from families that currently did not have psychiatric illness or were not seeking treatment. It was important to study parental affective disorder in a sample not recruited by referral for treatment. The incidence of affective disorder in the general population is higher than the number of individuals presenting for psychiatric treatment, and, thus, there may be differences in the nature of affective disorder in nonclinical samples that lead to different outcomes in the youngsters. There also may be differences in those who seek help and those who do not, or differences in the severity of affective disorder in referred and nonreferred samples.

A study was undertaken with the same rigorous methodology used in the study of clinical samples, but with families recruited from a local health maintenance organization (HMO), without knowledge of whether they had ever experienced affective disorders. The eventual sample included 153 youngsters from 81 families; approximately 80% of those contacted and eligible consented to participate. The eligibility criteria were the same as for the larger study (Beardslee and Podorefsky 1988). The overall study involved blind assessment of the parents with the Schedule of Affective Disorders and Schizophrenia and various other social functioning and demographic measures, assessment of the mother's view of the child's adaptive functioning and psychopathologic difficulties using standard instruments, and direct assessment of the youngsters about psychopathology, adaptive functioning, intellectual level, and various other parameters (Beardslee et al. 1985a, 1985b; Beardslee et al. 1987).

The HMO sample divided naturally into three main groups: 1) families in which parents had never experienced any psychiatric disorder (21 families with 45 children); 2) families in which parents had experienced nonaffective psychopathology only (11 families with 19 children); and 3) families in which one or both parents had experienced affective disorder, sometimes in combination with other illnesses (49 families with 89 children). There was considerable nonaffective psychopathology associated with the affective disorders. The most common diagnosis in the parents was major depressive disorder, followed by intermittent depressive disorder. The most common nonaffective diagnoses were alcoholism and various kinds of character pathology.

In terms of outcomes in the youngsters, there was a markedly increased rate of diagnoses in the children in families with parental disorder. Moreover, there was a specific effect of parental affective disorder on child affective disorder outcome. Two percent of children of parents without disorder experienced affective disorder, and none of the children of nonaffectively ill parents did, whereas 30% of the children of parents with affective disorder themselves had experienced affective disorder at some point before assessment. This finding was statistically significant. Children of parents with affective disorder had more diagnoses in numerous other serious categories, such as conduct disorder. This main effect of parental affective disorder on poor child outcome remained true when overall adaptive functioning was the outcome. Furthermore, the effect was not due to differences in age, sex, or IQ among the three groups. The data were reanalyzed, excluding all families experiencing divorce and separation, and the main effects were found to be statistically significant. The data were also reanalyzed using the family as the unit of analysis rather than the individual child, and the main effects also remained.

The specificity of the connection of affective disorder in parents with affective disorder in their children is striking. From a preventive viewpoint, although this study was done to explore the effects of parental affective disorder in a nonreferred sample and the main findings relate to that, it draws attention to another area as well: this is the first study to examine both parents and children with a diagnostic interview, blindly rated for subjects selected from an HMO. As such, it forms a complement to the increasingly sophisticated literature on the incidence and prevalence of psychiatric disorder in general medical practice. This study emphasizes that when parents have affective disorder in an HMO setting, youngsters are more likely to be ill, especially with affective disorder—in this sense, parental disorder is a marker for serious childhood disorder, especially depression, and thus has important clinical implications. This strongly emphasizes that concern about youngsters growing up in families with serious affective disorder should not be limited to families in which parents present clinically for the treatment of affective disorder, but that affective disorder when it occurs, referred or not, is of serious concern in terms of the greatly increased likelihood of poor child outcome. It also indicates more generally the link between parental mental illness and poor child outcome in nonreferred samples.

Resiliency

A striking finding in a wide variety of studies of youngsters at risk has been the considerable resiliency manifested by some subjects (Rutter 1986; Garmezy 1984; Anthony and Cohler 1987).

In these studies, positive interpersonal relationships have been found to be protective for children (Rutter 1986, 1979; Eisenberg 1979; Lieberman 1982), and they are characteristic of those who are resilient. Investigators have recognized the importance of other protective factors, both constitutional, such as certain temperamental characteristics (Porter and Collins 1982), and ways of responding, thinking, and acting, such as coping styles, positive sense of self, and control over one's surroundings (Garmezy 1983).

A recent study of resiliency in the children of parents with affective disorders attempted to identify dimensions that might be amenable to preventive intervention. This study focused on the youngsters' understandings of themselves, as this has proven important in other subject populations (Beardslee 1981, 1983). Eighteen youngsters were selected because of their good function from a group of more than 120, all of whose parents had experienced serious affective disorders (Beardslee and Podorefsky 1988). Examination of behavioral function and diagnoses was combined with an in-depth life-history interview 1.5–3 years after the initial cross-sectional interview.

The subjects' average age was 19 years at the second assessment. Fifteen of the 18 youngsters were functioning well at both points in time. These 15 youngsters had close confiding relationships with a wide variety of individuals, performed well in work and school, and had a wide variety of activities. Sixteen of the youngsters described themselves as valuing close confiding relationships and emphasized that these relationships were a central part of their lives. For many, relationships were crucial in allowing them to separate from their parents. Eleven of the young men and women assumed caretaking roles, either within the family or outside of it.

Their understandings of their parents' illnesses were remarkable. They were deeply aware of their parents' illnesses, had spent a great deal of time thinking about them, and had developed a considerable understanding. They were very clear that they were not the cause of their parents' disorders and were not to blame for them. They believed this understanding was crucial in their coping with the parental disorder. The actual disruption of their own lives, which was associated with or was a consequence of parental illness, was the focus of their accounts, rather than the identification of parents' behaviors as sequelae of depressions. The young people described major life events associated with parental illness in detail and often related the parental illness to the presence of painful life events. Especially important were parental divorce, deaths in the family, and, for a few, serious medical illnesses.

They were clearly able to distinguish between themselves (and their own experiences) and their parents' illnesses. They had reflected on their relationships and their experiences with their parents before the interview. They had somehow made peace with or come to an understanding of the experience that was important to them. More generally, they clearly saw themselves as separate, both from their parents' illness systems and from their parents, and indeed carried out independent actions. Three main components of self-understanding were identified through this and related studies:

1. Realistic appraisal of the stresses to be dealt with. In this case,

that involved the complex vicissitudes of the parental illness over time.
2. Realistic appraisal of the capacity to act and a sense of the importance and effect of one's actions.
3. Actions congruent with their view of their parents' and their own abilities.

Thus, self-understanding and separateness are psychological qualities associated with resiliency in the adolescent children of parents with affective disorder.

Mechanism

A genetic component to affective illness for both manic-depressive and depressive disorders has been demonstrated by the evidence from studies of monozygotic twins reared apart (Nurnberger and Gershon 1982) and by family studies that demonstrated that relatives of patients with affective disorder are at much higher risk for affective disorder themselves (Gershon et al. 1982). The mode of genetic transmission is unclear, and the relative weight of genetic factors as opposed to other risk factors remains to be elucidated.

Psychosocial stress factors, including increased rates of divorce and marital difficulty, frequent moves, diminished economic resources, and, most importantly, the inability of the parents to attend to and focus on the needs of the child, contribute to disorders in youngsters in families with serious affective disorder (Waters 1987; Beardslee 1984). These stresses are not specific to affective illness and characterize families with various parental mental disorders. Rutter and colleagues' (1974) analyses of the differences with respect to rates of childhood psychopathology between a London borough and the Isle of Wight have highlighted the importance of such nonspecific factors.

There may well be specific psychosocial factors in the transmission of illness from parent to child. Anthony (1977, 1983) has argued that certain specific cognitive and affective dissonances, especially in the mother, may be assimilated during development. The process of identification with the ill parent is also important (Anthony 1975). Attempts by the child to get inside the world of the ill parent to communicate with him or her may lead the child to take on some of the characteristics of the ill parent to see the world through the parent's eyes (Beardslee 1984).

The best overall integrative model for how various factors may come together has been proposed by Sameroff and Fiese (in press) in their work on prevention. They propose an interactive model in which both biological givens and parental societal factors influence the child initially. There is later a time when the child himself or herself has an influence on the parents, on his or her own subsequent development, and on the environment. Clearly, a combination of factors that interact and mutually influence one another are present, and the relative weight of such factors is not fully known. Over time, the factors of past experience and emerging biological competence also play important roles. Analysis of some of the dimensions involved in pathways of influence suggests that the largest single determinant of poor outcome in youngsters is serious affective disorder in the mother, although illness in the father, marital problems, social class, and certain factors in the child such as sex and past history of disorder are also important.

THE INTERVENTION—A COGNITIVE PSYCHOEDUCATIONAL APPROACH

In addition to the empirical data, clinical impressions gathered from extensive research and clinical work with these families support the need for intervention. Parents with affective disorders are very eager for help about how to deal with their youngsters. Almost always, families in my research project reported that they worried about the impact their illness had had on their youngsters and wanted help with their concerns. They indicated that they did not know what to do, or how even to think about the issue. It was also clear that the youngsters themselves did not understand the parents' illnesses and often felt guilty and blamed themselves for the disorder.

Although the data strongly point to the need for preventive intervention in families with serious affective disorder, as yet, programs for clinicians who treat parents with affective disorder have not been developed. [Editor's note: See also the third section of this book, "Approaches to Treating Families of Depressed Patients" (Chapters 6–9).] This lack is striking, because clinicians, whether in psychiatry, internal medicine, pediatrics, or similar disciplines, are often the first or main contact for an adult with serious affective disorder. The following protocol was developed to attempt to translate the findings about risk and resiliency into a standard measurable intervention that could be empirically tested for its effectiveness. The design of this intervention is aimed at teachableness to a wide variety of practitioners, not just those skilled in the intensive psychotherapeutic treatment or family-based treatment of serious disorders. In this sense, the intervention is more on a public health model and less on an intervention based on a particular school of psychotherapy.

A central issue in the intervention is the integration of different perspectives—biological, social, and family—in its design. From a clinician's point of view, the presentation of affective disorder is heterogeneous. Thus, a requirement for intervention is that it be flexible, in terms of the kind and nature of the explanation offered to the family and also the kinds of interventions possible. A central principle of this design of intervention is the belief that preventive intervention should be modeled to some extent on studies of resiliency—namely, what is found to be protective and helpful to youngsters who do well in the risk situation should then be developed in all youngsters.

In its present form, the intervention has been used in families in which parents have experienced a recent affective illness, often involving hospitalization, and in which the youngsters are in early to middle adolescence and are not yet ill. Although the protocol is described for a two-parent family, it can also be applied to a single-parent family.

The number of sessions is variable, with no more than 10 and no fewer than 6 sessions, and combines sessions involving parents alone, child (or children) alone, and parents and child (or children) together.

In its pilot form, the intervention has been conducted by a clinician separate from the person treating the parent's episodes of affective illness, although both functions could be carried out by the same individual.

Four main content areas are covered in the intervention: assessment, cognitive teaching, focus on the child's experience both present and future, and family discussion of the parent's illness.

Assessment

Initially, one or two parent-history sessions are held either with each spouse alone or with spouses together. A history of the parent's recent illness and past disorder, with a focus on each spouse's experience and understanding of it, is taken. Effects of the illness, particularly on the child, are explored. A brief assessment of how the child is functioning from the parents' points of view is obtained, along with screening for the presence of serious illness. Finally, parents are asked what concerns and questions they would like help with.

In sessions with children, the clinician explores the child's overall experience in school, with friends, in the family, and in outside activities and major symptoms if any are present. Concerns about the parent's illness, the child's experience of the parent's recent illness, and the child's questions are elicited.

Cognitive Teaching

In sessions with the parents alone, the clinician reviews what is known about the etiology of depression, its psychosocial manifestations, and the risks to children growing up in families with serious affective illness. The adaptive capacities of youngsters who function well in this and related risk situations are described.

Focus on Child Experience and Development of Plans for the Future

Sessions are conducted with both parents and specifically explore strategies that the family can use in discussing the parent's illness and planning for the future. The major areas covered include

1. Need for clarity on the child's part as to what has happened to the parent and to the family.
2. Provision to ensure that the child does not feel guilty or responsible.
3. Encouragement of the child's understanding of the nature of the illness, and that the parent's unavailability and incapacity need not limit the child.
4. Encouragement of explorations of networks of support for the child, particularly reestablishment of those that may have been disrupted by parental illness.
5. Discussion of difficulties the child may face.
6. Discussion of how to anticipate future development of illness in the child and seek prompt treatment.
7. Discussion of how to continue the ongoing process of understanding in the family. At the end of these sessions, the parents define together what they hope to accomplish in the family sessions with the children.

Family Sessions—Discussion of the Parent's Illness

Two family sessions are held to present this material to the child or children. It is made clear to the child that he or she is not to blame. There is discussion about how the child can understand various things that have happened to the parent. The child is encouraged to ask questions about anything that has been discussed. Plans for the future are discussed in terms of continued exploration of the issue and also in terms of any specific concerns that have come up.

In instances where clear diagnosable disorders requiring treatment in youngsters or the spouse are identified, referral for treatment is made. Help with referral, should difficulties develop in the future, is offered by the clinician.

After the intervention, the clinician is available to the family by telephone as needed and meets with the family at 6 and 12 months to review both the intervention and what has happened since the intervention in terms of understanding of parental illness and difficulties youngsters may have had to face.

CLINICAL EXPERIENCE

In eliciting histories, I have found it useful to ask parents to describe not only what their own histories have been, but also how they think the children have experienced those histories. This lays the groundwork for the parents to take the perspective of the youngster early on in the intervention and, indeed, see the world from the youngster's eyes. It also often elicits information quite different from a traditional psychiatric history.

In terms of cognitive teaching, it has been useful to use the analogy of a heart attack and to try to get first the parents and then the family to understand that having a depression is a serious medical illness, like a heart attack, which has medical consequences and requires a change in physical and emotional activity. However, it is explainable, not mystical, and no one is to blame for it.

In working with the youngsters themselves, I have tried to elicit what their actual experience has been and also what their concerns are, particularly their unanswered questions or fears for the future. This also lays a groundwork for family understanding through family sessions.

If it is a two-parent family, it is important for the couple to work together. The overall aim of the intervention, in addition to transmitting information and identifying disorder, is to share a perspective with the parents; that is, to enable them to think about the world through their children's eyes and, based on this, to enter into a dialogue with their children. This process is far more important than any final single cognitive answer or way of explaining what actually happened. This is because, clearly, the youngsters, over a longer period than the time of the intervention, will wrestle with and try to come to grips with what the parent's disorder has been. They and the parents need to be able to talk about this over time. For example, some youngsters undergo anniversary reactions at the actual date or time of the parent's hospitalization in the previous year. Sensitivity to this can help them deal with it.

Furthermore, it is important to start from what the direct parental concerns are. In the pilot family, after I explained the intervention to the mother and started to outline general principles, she said, "I have two main concerns. I had electroconvulsive therapy and I have intense short-term memory loss. I can't remember things from one day to the next. I don't know how to explain this to my children. Secondly, I did feel like killing myself before I went into the hospital, and I don't know how to explain this to my children." At this point, it was essential to deal directly with these concerns, rather than continuing with the original agenda.

In a complementary way, it is very important to know as much as possible of what the youngsters have actually experienced. In the illustration above, both the electroconvulsive therapy and the sequelae were well known to the youngsters and could be dealt with directly. It turned out that thoughts about suicide were less explicit and were dealt with differently. In this connection, it has generally proven to be important to say more rather than less in cognitive terms. It is more useful for parents to go ahead and say to the children, for example, "You are not guilty and you are not to blame for what happened," even if the youngster has not said, "I feel guilty or to blame." The experience of youngsters so often is that they feel they are the cause of their parents' illnesses and it is important to address this directly.

More generally, it is essential that the persons intervening with these families recognize their role in trying to demystify what has often been a complex and overwhelming event for the child. It is important to help the child see that the event is not overwhelming, but can be understood, both cognitively and emotionally, and that a framework of dialogue and understanding between parent and child is possible. An important consideration is the issue of whether parental behavior is understood as continuous or discontinuous with normal living. In contrast to frank psychosis, depression usually is episodic, insidious, and somewhat continuous with normal behavior. A mother or father may become increasingly irritable or increasingly preoccupied without a clear-cut precipitant. Individuals become impaired slowly and gradually. In the beginning, a parent's withdrawal, sadness, crying, or irritability may be attributed by the child to his or her failure or acting out. For a time, that explanation may become part of his or her worldview. It is essential to break through this to provide a different explanation and to emphasize that the behavior in depression is really discontinuous from normal behavior. It is not the way the parents want to be; there is an alternative framework of understanding and the child need not be responsible or blame himself or herself.

Finally, two other perspectives have proven useful. First, it is important for clinicians to recognize that doing preventive intervention is very different from treating known disorder with known proven methods. It means venturing into the unknown, as the future, indeed, is unknown. It means moving away from a sense of certainty of clear-cut diagnosis and appropriate treatment to a sense of building on known strengths, identifying risk factors, and helping the family think and plan for the future. This requires considerable rethinking on the clinician's part.

Second, all kinds of fears, concerns, and unspoken guilts are part of serious mental illness. In our society, we do not treat serious mental illness in the way we treat physical illness. Parents themselves are quite prone to feel terribly guilty, to be ashamed, and to blame themselves for mental illness. They are often very ashamed of talking about the depression or even mentioning that they have been treated or hospitalized. Their youngsters sense this. A clinician intervening must be honest, responsible, and, above all, open to talking about anything that concerns the parent or child about the illness. The clinician must be flexible in dealing with it and demonstrate that he or she is not thrown by it or overwhelmed by it. The example of how the clinician deals with the material serves as a model for the family and helps break through the social stigma so often attached to serious affective disorder.

REFERENCES

Anthony EJ: The influence of a manic-depressive environment on the developing child, in Depression and Human Existence. Edited by Anthony EJ, Benedek T. Boston, MA, Little, Brown, 1975

Anthony EJ: Preventive measures for children and adolescents at high risk for psychosis, in Primary Prevention of Psychopathology, Vol II: The Issues. Edited by Albee GW, Joffee JM. Hanover, NH, University Press of New England, 1977

Anthony EJ: The preventive approach to children at high risk for psychopathology and psychosis. Journal of Children in Contemporary Society 15:67–72, 1983

Anthony EJ, Cohler BJ (eds): The Invulnerable Child. New York, Clifford, 1987

Beardslee WR: Self-understanding and coping with cancer, in The Damocles Syndrome: Psychosocial Consequences of Surviving Childhood Cancer. Edited by Koocher GP, O'Malley JE. New York, McGraw-Hill, 1981

Beardslee WR: The Way Out Must Lead In: Life Histories in the Civil Rights Movement, 2nd ed. Westport, CT, Lawrence Hill, 1983

Beardslee WR: Familial influences in childhood depression. Pediatr Ann 13:32–36, 1984

Beardslee WR, Podorefsky D: Resilient adolescents whose parents have serious affective and other psychiatric disorders: importance of self-understanding and relationships. Am J Psychiatry 145:63–69, 1988

Beardslee WR, Keller MB, Klerman GL: Children of parents with affective disorder. International Journal of Family Psychiatry 6:283–299, 1985a

Beardslee WR, Klerman GL, Keller MB, et al: But are they cases? Validity of DSM-III major depression in children identified in family study. Am J Psychiatry 142:687–691, 1985b

Beardslee WR, Schultz LH, Selman RL: Level of social-cognitive development, adaptive functioning, and DSM-III diagnoses in adolescent offspring of parents with affective disorders: implications of the development of the capacity for mutuality. Developmental Psychology 23:807–815, 1987

Berrueta-Clement J, Schweinhar L, Barnett W, et al: Changed Lives: The Effect of the Perry Preschool Program on Youths Through Age 19. Ypsilanti, MI, High/Scope Press, 1985

Chandler CL, Weissberg RP, Cowen EL, et al: Long-term effects of a school-based secondary prevention program for young maladapting children. J Consult Clin Psychol 52:165–170, 1984

Chassin LA, Presson CC, Sherman SJ: Stepping backward in order to step forward: an acquisition oriented approach to primary prevention. J Consult Clin Psychol 53:612–622, 1985

Cytryn L, McKnew DH, Bartko JJ, et al: Offspring of patients with affective disorders: II. J Am Acad Child Psychiatry 21:389–391, 1982

Earls F: Toward the prevention of psychiatric disorders, in Psychiatry Update: American Psychiatric Association Annual Review, Vol 6. Edited by Hales RE, Frances AJ. Washington, DC, American Psychiatric Press, 1987

Eisenberg L: A friend, not an apple, a day will help keep the doctor away. Am J Med 66:551–553, 1979

Eisenberg L: A research framework for evaluating the promotion of mental health and prevention of mental illness. Prevention of Mental Illness 96:3–19, 1981

Eisenberg L: Prevention: rhetoric and reality. Journal of the Royal Society of Medicine 77:268–280, 1984

Falloon IRH, McGill CW, Boyd JL, et al: Family management in the prevention of morbidity of schizophrenia: social outcome of a two-year longitudinal study. Psychol Med 17:59–66, 1987

Garmezy N: Stressors of childhood, in Stress, Coping and Development in Children. Edited by Garmezy N, Rutter M. New York, McGraw-Hill, 1983

Garmezy N: Children vulnerable to major mental disorders: risk and protective factors, in Psychiatry Update, Vol III. Edited by Grinspoon L. Washington, DC, American Psychiatric Press, 1984

Gershon ES, Hamovit J, Gunroff JJ, et al: A family study of schizoaffective bipolar I, bipolar II, unipolar, and normal control probands. Arch Gen Psychiatry 39:1157–1167, 1982

Ginsburg SD, Twentyman CT: Prevention of childhood depression, in Depression Prevention. Edited by Munoz RF. New York, Hemisphere, 1987

Grunebaum H: Parenting and children at risk, in Psychiatry Update: The American Psychiatric Association Annual Review, Vol 3. Edited by Grinspoon L. Washington, DC, American Psychiatric Press, 1984

Keller MB, Klerman GL, Lavori PW, et al: Treatment received by depressed patients. JAMA 16:229–240, 1982

Keller MB, Lavori PW, Endicott J, et al: Double depression: a two-year follow-up. Am J Psychiatry 6:689–694, 1983

Keller MB, Beardslee WR, Dorer DJ, et al: Impact of severity and chronicity of parental affective illness on adaptive functioning and psychopathology in their children. Arch Gen Psychiatry 43:930–937, 1986

Keller MB, Beardslee WR, Lavori PW, et al: Course of major depression in nonreferred adolescents: a retrospective study. J Affective Disord (in press)

Kolvin I, Garside RF, Nicol AR, et al (eds): Help Starts Here: The Maladjusted Child in the Ordinary School. London, Tavistock, 1981

Kovacs M, Feinberg TL, Crouse-Novak MA, et al: Depressive disorders in childhood, I: a longitudinal approach. Arch Gen Psychiatry 41:229–287, 1984

Lazar I, Darlington B: Lasting effects of early education: a report from the Consortium for Longitudinal Studies. Monogr Soc Res Child Dev 47 (2–3, Serial No. 195), 1982

Lewinsohn PM: The coping-with-depression course, in Depression Prevention: Research Directions. Edited by Munoz RF. New York, Hemisphere, 1987

Lieberman MA: The effects of social supports on response to stress, in Handbook of Stress: Theoretical and Clinical Aspects. Edited by Golberge L, Breznit S. New York, Free Press, 1982

McKey RH, Condelli L, Ganson H, et al: The impact of Head Start on children, family and communities: final report of the Head Start Evaluation Synthesis and Utilization Project (DHHS Publication No OHDS 85–31193). Washington, DC, U.S. Government Printing Office, 1985

Merikangas KR: Divorce and assortative mating among depressed patients. Am J Psychiatry 141:75–76, 1984

Munoz RF: Depression prevention research: conceptual and practical considerations, in Depression Prevention. Edited by Munoz RF. New York, Hemisphere, 1987

Munoz RF, Ying YW, Armas R, et al: The San Francisco depression prevention research project, in Depression Prevention. Edited by Munoz RF. New York, Hemisphere, 1987

Nurnberger JI, Gershon ES: Genetics of affective disorder, in Handbook of Affective Disorders. Edited by Paykel ES. New York, Guilford Press, 1982

Philips I: Opportunities for prevention in the practice of psychiatry. Am J Psychiatry 140:389–395, 1983

Porter R, Collins GM (eds): Temperamental difference in infants and young children. Ciba Found Symp 89, London, Pitman, 1982

Rehm LP: Approaches to the prevention of depression with children: a self-management perspective, in Depression Prevention. Edited by Munoz RF. New York, Hemisphere, 1987

Rolf JE: Evolving adaptive theories and methods for prevention research with children. J Consult Clin Psychol 53:631–646, 1985

Rush AJ (ed): Short-Term Psychotherapies for Depression. New York, Guilford Press, 1987

Rutter M: Protective factors in children's response to stress and disadvantage, in Primary Prevention of Psychopathology, Vol III: Social Competence in Children. Edited by Rolf R, Kent MD. Hanover, NH, University Press of New England, 1979

Rutter M: Prevention of children's psychosocial disorders: myth and substance. Pediatrics 70:883–894, 1982

Rutter M: Meyerian psychobiology, personality development, and the role of life experiences. Am J Psychiatry 143:1077–1087, 1986

Rutter M, Yule B, Quinton D, et al: Attainment and adjustment in two geographical areas, III: some factors accounting for area differences. Br J Psychiatry 125:520–533, 1974

Sameroff AJ, Fiese BH: Transactional regulation and early interaction, in Early Intervention: A Handbook of Theory, Practice and Analysis. Edited by Meisels SJ, Shonkoff JP. Cambridge, MA, Cambridge University Press (in press)

Spaulding J, Balch P: A brief history of primary prevention in the twentieth century: 1908 to 1980. Am J Community Psychol 11:59–80, 1983

Vega WA, Valle R, Kolody B, et al: The Hispanic social network prevention intervention study: a community-based randomized trial, in Depression Prevention. Edited by Munoz RF. New York, Hemisphere, 1987

Waters BG: Psychiatric disorders in the offspring of parents with affective disorder: a review. Journal of Preventive Psychiatry 3:191–206, 1987

Weissman MM, Myers JR: Affective disorders in a U.S. urban community. Arch Gen Psychiatry 35:1304–1311, 1987

Weissman MM, Prusoff BA, Gammon GD, et al: Psychopathology in the children (ages 6–18) of depressed and normal parents. J Am Acad Child Psychiatry 23:78–84, 1984a

Weissman MM, Leckman JF, Merikangas KR, et al: Depression and anxiety disorders in parents and children. Arch Gen Psychiatry 41:845–852, 1984b

Welner Z, Garrison WT: Blind high-risk study of depressives' offspring: preliminary data. International Journal of Family Psychiatry 6:301–314, 1985

Welner Z, Welner A, McCrary MD, et al: Psychopathology in children of inpatients with depression: a controlled study. J Nerv Ment Dis 164:408–413, 1977

Zigler EF, Valentine J: Project Head Start: A Legacy of the War on Poverty. New York, Free Press, 1979

Zuckerman BS, Beardslee WR: Maternal depression: a concern for pediatricians. Pediatrics 79:110–117, 1987

Chapter 6

Inpatient Family Intervention for Affective Disorders

John F. Clarkin, Ph.D.
Ira D. Glick, M.D.
Gretchen L. Haas, Ph.D.
James H. Spencer, Jr., M.D.

Chapter 6

Inpatient Family Intervention for Affective Disorders

Two hallmarks of state-of-the-art psychotherapy research are the definition of a model of the target disorder or pathology and the implementation of a manualized therapy that is focused on altering the course or outcome of the condition. We have constructed and investigated the effects of a manualized inpatient family intervention package on patients with major affective disorder, schizophrenia, and other major psychiatric disorders at the point at which they require hospitalization. The focus of this chapter is on the design and outcome of a clinical trial of this inpatient family intervention for patients with major affective disorder and their families.

The design of Inpatient Family Intervention for Affective Disorders—IFI (AD)—was influenced by the nature of affective disorders in several ways. IFI was constructed to provide information (psychoeducation) to the patient and the family about the symptoms, course, and treatment of affective disorders. It was hypothesized that with this information the family could better plan for the appropriate treatment of the patient posthospitalization. Second, because affective disorder is considered stress responsive, the family intervention was directed to assist the family in reducing potential future family stressors as well as to help them cope with the stress of the immediate hospitalization.

Interestingly enough, we had little prior literature from which to draw in the construction of a family intervention for patients hospitalized with an affective disorder. Although the utilization of family intervention in inpatient settings has expanded exponentially, this growth has not been matched by clinical research. Before our work at the Payne Whitney Clinic in New York City, there had been no controlled study of family intervention on an inpatient service. Of the two relevant inpatient studies, one was not well controlled and was limited to adolescents (Wellisch et al. 1976), and the other involved the family as a minor component in a social skills training program for schizophrenic patients (Wallace and Liberman 1985). In addition, there was very limited research on the influence of marital/family therapy on the course of affective disorder. Friedman (1975) studied the outpatient marital treatment of couples in which one partner was depressed. Davenport and Adland (1988) reported on the benefits of a group marital therapy for couples in which one partner had a bipolar disorder.

Our own approach evolved out of daily inpatient work with severely disturbed patients and their families. The only previous research work that seemed relevant to our orientation and daily functioning was that reported by Goldstein et al. (1978) on schizophrenic patients and their families on an outpatient basis.

MODELS OF AFFECTIVE DISORDER AND THE FAMILY CONTEXT

The prevailing models of affective disorder include psychosocial variables in the etiology and course of the disorder (e.g., Haas et al. 1985; Billings and Moos 1985; Brown and Harris 1978) and give credence to the development of a family intervention model. These models are explicated elsewhere, but the essential points will be summarized here:

1. Marital and family functioning are particularly affected by depressive episodes in a member. There is less problem-solving behavior and less self-disclosure in couples with a depressed member (Biglan et al., in press). Interpersonal friction, poor communication, and diminished sexual satisfaction characterize marriages in which one spouse is depressed (Rounsaville et al. 1979; Weissman and Paykel 1974).
2. High levels of stress are associated with low social support in those who experience depression. Depressed individuals seek more social support than others and perceive themselves as receiving less (Coyne et al. 1981; Schaefer et al. 1981).
3. The coping styles of depressed individuals are characterized by poor effectiveness, seeking of emotional or informational support, wishful thinking, and negative self-preoccupation (Coyne et al. 1981; Folkman and Lazarus 1986).
4. Many bipolar patients are difficult to treat, often denying the need for medication or acknowledging only the biochemistry of the illness that can be cured with a pill. The episodes of manic behavior are often characterized by alienated and destructive interpersonal

behavior, especially within the family system (Davenport and Adland 1988).

SPECIFIC AIMS OF FAMILY INTERVENTION

Given the association between family environmental stress and affective disorder, coupled with the growing evidence that family intervention can be helpful in the course of a major psychiatric condition such as schizophrenia (Falloon et al. 1982), we hypothesized that a brief inpatient family intervention would be clinically useful for patients with major affective disorders. Hypotheses were formulated concerning the mechanism of action and the role of specific treatment and final goals of intervention. The accomplishment of the specific targeted treatment goals of IFI was expected to lead to improved family attitudes toward the patient and toward use of mental health services in the future. In addition, it was hypothesized that positive family attitudes toward treatment would promote patient compliance with aftercare pharmacological and psychosocial treatment, the latter (i.e., aftercare) contributing to overall better functioning and an improved symptom picture for the patient.

In designing an inpatient family intervention, we had only modest goals in mind. After all, we were using a brief family intervention, limited to the hospitalization phase, with no control over outpatient follow-up. In addition, we were dealing with patients whose pathology (affective and associated Axis II conditions) was severe enough to occasion a psychiatric hospitalization. The affective pathology was probably caused in varying degrees by biological factors not under the direct influence of family intervention.

It is difficult to demonstrate an incremental effect of treatment added (in this case, IFI) to hospitalization for patients with an acute disorder. Inpatients often show substantial improvement related to the change of environment via hospitalization, medication, and passage of time. Because both groups (IFI and non-IFI) received extensive hospital treatment including medication, milieu treatment, and individual treatment, simply adding IFI might not show a robust incremental effect. However, despite these difficulties, we decided to use this "constructive," i.e., add-on, design because it reflected typical clinical practice. Many hospitals across the country have added brief family intervention to the array of interventions typically used. The practical question for the clinicians at these sites concerns the effectiveness of adding a family intervention module. In this chapter, we present data bearing on the specific utility for treatment of patients with major affective disorders.

DESCRIPTION OF OUR FAMILY TREATMENT MODEL

IFI is a brief, psychoeducational, problem-focused family treatment structured to assist the patient and family in coping with the hospitalization of a family member. IFI is called family "intervention" rather than family "therapy" because the latter term carries connotations that are often not applicable to work in an inpatient setting.

Assumptions

Our family treatment model assumes that the affective episode is not caused by family environment or family communication problems. Although greatly influenced by psychosocial factors, these disorders are partly biological in nature. Thus, we do not assume that the manic or depressive symptoms are under exclusive or even predominant control of the repetitive family interaction patterns. Furthermore, one cannot infer that the family interaction patterns seen at the time of the hospitalization are typical, or that such patterns of interaction caused or even maintained the symptomatic behavior in the identified patient. More often than not, the family is doing what it perceives as necessary at that point in time to cope with the situation. This assumption assists the clinician in establishing an alliance with the family by reducing attitudes of blame toward the family.

It is assumed that the provision of information about the affective disorder will enable the family to use its own strengths in coping with the condition. The process of providing information itself can be instrumental in building a therapeutic alliance with the family and in working through basic maladaptive attitudes toward the disturbed family member. This process can also promote more effective use of the mental health treatment system during and after hospitalization. Some families will not be reached by such a straightforward process, but the attempt will further strengthen therapy by pushing the limits of such an approach.

It is assumed that the crisis period of hospitalization is not the time to rehash long-standing family and marital conflicts. Such conflicts may or may not be related to the affective episode, and, therefore, focusing on these is not a first priority. For some families, however, the crisis of hospitalization may be a powerful impetus to major change in established family patterns. The first priority is for the clinician to take an active role in directing the dialogue away from intense emotional turmoil and long-standing family conflict or blame for the patient's episode. The task is to deal with issues and matters at hand: What immediate crises and/or difficulties preceded the hospitalization? What is the family's understanding of the nature and prognosis of affective disorder? What treatment will be needed on discharge from the hospital, and will the family and patient accept this?

Treatment Goals of IFI

Six treatment goals define and guide the orientation of IFI:

1. Helping the patient and family to accept the reality of the affective disorder and to develop an understanding of the current episode
2. Identifying possible precipitating stresses relevant to the current episode
3. Identifying likely future stresses both within and outside of the family
4. Elucidating the family interaction sequences that produce stress on the identified patient
5. Planning strategies to manage or minimize future stresses
6. Educating the patient and family regarding the nature of the treatment and the need for continued treatment after discharge from the hospital

The six goals of IFI were pursued differentially depending on the existing problems and the specific needs of each family. The family therapist and the supervisor set the goals for each case at the beginning of treatment, and at the time of discharge the family therapist rated the extent to which each goal was achieved.

Therapeutic Strategies of IFI

We have elsewhere (Clarkin et al. 1981) delineated in detail treatment strategies and techniques to assist in achieving these six goals. In general, the strategies involved 1) psychoeducation, 2) exploration and clarification about specific family stressors on the patient, 3) problem solving around managing the stressors, and 4) planning for aftercare. This was *not* behavioral family therapy, in the sense that we did not role-play or practice family communication skills and problem-solving behavior. There was not enough time to accomplish such labor-intensive behavior rehearsal strategies. Furthermore, there was less emphasis on psychodynamic or structural family therapy strategies. These strategies were seen as too invasive for a brief intervention in the context of hospitalization for a severely debilitating disorder. Our strategies were more akin to those of interpersonal therapy (Klerman et al. 1984). For example, the patient was viewed as occupying the "sick role" (by virtue of being hospitalized); there was assessment and discussion of stress and conflict in the family environment. Disposition planning for families in need of more extensive behavioral and/or structural family treatment included referrals for outpatient family therapy.

Family Clinicians

The family clinicians in our study were social workers who had had previous family therapy experience with inpatients and their families. The social workers were often accompanied in the family work by second-year psychiatric residents and first-year psychology interns who also served as primary therapists for the patients. The family clinicians were comfortable with the goals and strategies of IFI and helped formulate the specific interventions. Cases were presented periodically for group discussion and supervision, and many families were interviewed in a group setting to begin the focus of IFI.

EMPIRICAL INVESTIGATION OF IFI

Patients and Their Families

Patients with major affective disorders by DSM-III admitted consecutively to a metropolitan psychiatric hospital were screened for admission to the study with the following criteria: 1) a minimum age of 18, 2) availability of family or significant others for family intervention, and 3) an anticipated length of stay sufficient for a minimum of six sessions of family intervention. In all, 297 patients met study criteria. Of these, 111 patients refused informed consent, leaving 186 patients who entered the study. Of these 186 consenting patients, 50 patients met criteria for an affective disorder.

The bipolar patients ($n = 21$) were predominantly white (81%) and female (67%) with a mean age of 32. Marital status was quite varied, with 52% single, 33% married, and 14% divorced. Forty-eight percent had no previous hospitalizations, and 33% had no previous episodes of illness. There was a more seriously disturbed subgroup (14%) with three or more previous hospitalizations, and 19% with three or more previous bipolar episodes.

The unipolar patients ($n = 29$) were predominantly white (62%), with almost equal distribution of men (45%) and women (55%). The mean age was 38. Thirty-one percent of the patients were single, 52% married, and 17% divorced or separated. Sixty-two percent of the patients had no previous hospitalizations, and 48% had no previous episodes. In contrast, 14% had experienced three or more previous hospitalizations and three or more previous episodes.

Within the first week of admission to the hospital, all patients (and their families) who satisfied the selection criteria and consented to participate in the study were randomly assigned to either multimodal hospital treatment with IFI or multimodal hospital treatment without IFI (the "comparison treatment" condition). The standard hospital treatment included medication when indicated, individual sessions with a primary therapist, and group and milieu treatment. Twelve bipolar patients received IFI and 9 received the comparison treatment; 17 unipolar patients were randomized to IFI and 12 received comparison treatment.

Assessment and Statistical Analysis Procedures

The study design included three independent variables: treatment assignment (hospitalization with IFI or hospitalization without IFI), diagnosis (unipolar or bipolar affective disorder), and sex. There were three dependent patient variables: global outcome, symptomatology, and role functioning; and two dependent family variables: family attitude toward treatment and social support and attitude toward patient/family burden.

Numerous instruments were used to assess the dependent variables. (See Glick et al. 1985; Haas et al. 1988, for additional details.) These included ratings of patient global functioning (Global Assessment Scale [GAS] ratings by independent rater), symptomatology (Psychiatric Evaluation Form [PEF] by independent rater), role functioning (PEF by independent rater), treatment compliance (Role Performance and Treatment Scale [RPTS] ratings by independent rater), and family attitudes toward the patient, toward treatment for the patient, and toward the burden the patient exerts (self-report by significant family members on the Family Attitude Scale [FAS]). Family therapists rated the accomplishment of the family treatment goals.

Because Type I errors may occur when multiple tests of significance are performed on multiple outcome measures, a principal components analysis was used to reduce the individual measures to composite outcome scores. We will report here on the two patient composite scores that emerged from the data. The patient composite scores were global functioning and symptoms (PCOMP1) and role functioning (PCOMP2). PCOMP1 was a composite score generated by GAS, PEF overall score, and PEF summary scales of grandiosity, disorganization, withdrawal, and subjective distress. PCOMP2 was a composite score from the RPTS role-functioning scales concerning primary role, family, social, and leisure activities. The two family composite scores were attitude to treatment/social support (FCOMP1) and attitude to patient/family burden (FCOMP2). FCOMP1 was a composite score from the FAS Factor 2, attitude toward treatment, and FAS Factor 5, openness to social support. FCOMP2 was composed of FAS Factor 1, attitude toward the patient, and FAS Factor 4, family burden. We used higher-order analyses of covariance with composite outcome measures to minimize both Type I and Type II errors. Table 1 summarizes the positive trends and significant results on these composite scores for the total sample of patients with affective disorder.

Outcome for All Patients With Affective Disorder

Women with affective disorder who underwent IFI did significantly better on the composite symptomatology/global outcome measure (PCOMP1) than those in the comparison group at discharge; on the other hand, men with affective disorder were little affected. Role functioning (PCOMP2) was not measured at discharge because the patients had not yet returned to family and community roles. Family attitude toward treatment was significantly better in women who underwent IFI than in comparison women, whereas family attitude toward the patient was significantly better in men who received the comparison treatment than in men who received IFI.

At 6- and 18-month follow-up, PCOMP1 and PCOMP2 did not show a main effect of treatment for all patients with affective disorder. Likewise, there were no main effects of treatment on either of the two family composite measures for the total affective group.

Table 1. Results of analyses at 6 and 18 months on composite patient and family measures for total affective disorder sample

	6 months		18 months	
	Independent variable	*P*	Independent variable	*P*
Patient global functioning/ symptoms (PCOMP1)	TAxDX	.09	TAxDX	.05
Patient role functioning (PCOMP2)	TAxDX	.02	TAxDX	.001
Family attitude to treatment/social support (FCOMP1)				
Family attitude to patient/family burden (FCOMP2)	TAxDX	.04		

Note. $N = 50$. TA = treatment assignment; DX = diagnosis.

Outcome by Subdiagnosis

One of the foci of this investigation was the differential effectiveness of family intervention during a hospitalization episode on patients of varying subdiagnoses. IFI was designed as a general family intervention, and there was no a priori reason to expect differential outcome for unipolar and bipolar patients irrespective of severity of condition. To our surprise, IFI had a significant beneficial effect on bipolar patients but had a negative effect on unipolar patients. At both 6 and 18 months, bipolar patients showed better outcome with IFI, whereas unipolar patients did better without it. On PCOMP1, there was a treatment by subdiagnosis trend that became significant at 18 months. It is clear from inspection of composite means that the patients with bipolar illness did better with IFI, whereas unipolar patients did better with the comparison treatment. As will be discussed further in a later section of this chapter on sex effects, the bipolar treatment effect was due to female patients only, whereas the negative effect on unipolar patients appeared in both sexes.

On PCOMP2, there was a significant interaction of treatment with subdiagnosis at 6- and 18-month follow-up. Again, the bipolar patients did better with IFI, and the unipolar patients did better with the comparison treatment.

On FCOMP2, attitude to patient/family burden, there was a treatment by subdiagnosis interaction effect at 6-month follow-up, again favoring the IFI bipolar patients.

Why did IFI favorably affect bipolar patients and unfavorably affect unipolar patients? Was it due to the affective subdiagnosis itself, or to some variable(s) correlated with subdiagnosis? Unfortunately, the answers to these questions are not clear with these results. As will be noted with more detail in further sections of this chapter, the subdiagnosis is confounded in this study with sex differences. However, the bipolar and unipolar groups were not significantly different at baseline on such potentially important variables as socioeconomic status, prior functioning, indices of severity of illness, incidence of severe personality disorder, history of prior treatment compliance, and treatment compliance after hospitalization.

Alternatively, it could be argued that although the general goals of IFI are equally appropriate for both bipolar and unipolar patients, in this study the goals may have been somewhat differentially applied to each of the two diagnostic subgroups because the clinician determined at her discretion the differential application and weight of the six goals of IFI depending on the specifics of the individual patient and family. We assessed this possibility and found that the relative emphasis on each of the six IFI goals was roughly equivalent for bipolar and unipolar patients and their families. Also significant was the finding that achievement of the goals—as rated by the family clinicians—was equivalent for the two diagnostic subgroups.

Outcome by Sex

As with the major affective disorder subdiagnosis, there was no a priori reason to anticipate sex differences in response to IFI. However, sex differences did emerge rather prominently in the empirical results. [Editor's note: For another discussion of sex differences in responding to depressive disorder, see Chapter 1.] At discharge from the index hospitalization, the most striking beneficial effect of IFI was on women with affective disorders. For unipolar patients, there was a treatment by sex trend on FCOMP1 at 6 months, and on FCOMP2, there was a treatment by sex trend at 18 months. In both instances, families of male patients were showing a negative effect of IFI.

Outcome Related to Sex by Subdiagnosis

Sex and subdiagnosis are somewhat confounded in our study because the bipolar IFI sample contained a higher percentage of women than did the unipolar group. Within the bipolar group, the positive effect of IFI is seen dramatically in the female patients and not at all in the male patients.

Outcome Across Time

After an average hospital stay of 47.5 days (SD = 27.7), results at discharge showed differential effectiveness of IFI, with a positive treatment effect specific to female patients with affective disorder. The families' attitudes toward treatment were significantly better in the IFI female patients than in the comparison female patients. In contrast, family attitude toward the patient was significantly better in comparison treatment male patients than in the IFI male patients. Given that IFI was extremely brief (average number of sessions was six) and that the design was such that all patients got potent treatments, it is noteworthy that we got significant results at the point of discharge. As mentioned before, IFI was an add-on treatment to the multiple treatments of hospitalization and cannot be expected to carry a major weight of the outcome variance even at discharge, let alone at follow-up points. If there were no effects at discharge, one would wonder about the contribution of IFI.

Given the demonstrated effect of IFI on some patients by time of discharge, one can then examine the data for potential continued or even enhanced effects over time. In this design, we did not control for aftercare, nor did we include IFI on discharge for a subsample. Over time, the initial effect of IFI demonstrated by time of discharge tended to diminish. At both follow-up points, there was no main effect of treatment on patient or family composite scores. There were, however, some interaction effects that persisted over time. At 6 months, there was a treatment by subdiagnosis trend that was significant at 18 months, showing that on PCOMP1 bipolar patients did better with IFI, whereas unipolar patients did better with a comparison treatment. On PCOMP2, there was a significant interaction of treatment with subdiagnosis at both follow-up points. Once again, the bipolar patients did better with IFI and the unipolar patients with the comparison treatment. Likewise, on FCOMP2, the family attitude toward patient/family burden yielded a treatment by subdiagnosis interaction effect at 6 months, with bipolar families having a better outcome with IFI and unipolar families a better outcome with the comparison treatment.

FUTURE RESEARCH

In an effort to inform future research efforts, we will briefly discuss problems in the design of the current study and methods for improving on similar study designs.

In this study, we were not able to consistently monitor the therapeutic intervention. Optimally, this would have been done by videotaping a sample of the therapy sessions, which would have been helpful in ensuring consistency and competency in the delivery of the treatment. We are impressed with the recent literature that suggests substantial individual therapist variance (e.g., Luborsky et al. 1986) and the therapist's deficient skills and/or decreased competence when faced with patients (and probably more so, families) who are hostile toward the therapist or the therapy itself.

It seems clear that assessment of the progress toward achieving mediating goals of family intervention is problematic and lacks any well-defined and valid methodology at present. The typical mediating goals of most family interventions involve some change in family interaction patterns related to problematic or symptomatic situations (e.g., parental reactions to depressive withdrawal). In our investigation, the identification and measurement of mediating goals included assessment of key family members' attitudes toward the patient, the illness, the family's burden with the illness, and the need for further treatment. We have no direct evidence that these attitudes correlate with key behaviors within or outside of the treatment context. In addition, there are probably other key behaviors of family members that significantly influence the patient and his or her progress—behavioral dimensions that we did not measure in this study. Future studies of actual patient-family interactions may assist in targeting intervention and measuring pre- and posttreatment changes.

We are impressed with the heterogeneity of the patients who met DSM-III criteria for major affective disorder. Whereas the patients were homogeneous to Axis I affective criteria, they were heterogeneous to Axis II, IV, and V and other nondiagnostic patient variables. Unfortunately, we did not have a reliable diagnosis of the Axis II pathology for the patients included in this study. Prior research suggests that an affective disorder group would have a substantial number of individuals with coexisting personality pathology. It is our impression that the personality disorders of both patient and family members heavily influenced both the receptivity to and the issues raised by the IFI sessions.

As family therapists, we are also impressed with the heterogeneity of the families of the patients. [Editor's note: For a further discussion on the heterogeneity of families of depressed patients, see Chapter 1.] This was a heterogeneity that existed on many levels. Family composition (e.g., single parent, parents, and sibs) and developmental stage (e.g., young adult with parents, patient and spouse) were variable. There was also wide variation in the personal adjustment of the individual family members. If a GAS score was done on each family member, the range of scores could conceivably be as wide as that of the patients themselves. More directly, there was wide variation between and within families along dimensions of acceptance-rejection of the patient, denial-acceptance of the mental disorder, low to high perceived burden in relation to the patient and the illness, etc. We have some documentation of this variability in the range of family attitude scores (on the FAS) toward the patient, his or her disorder, and the need for treatment.

In future studies, there will be greater specification and measurement of these important family variables, all of which singly and collectively could contribute to the course of the patient's disorder and recovery.

Other important nondiagnostic patient and family variables may influence or modify patient and family outcome, including prior treatment compliance, sex of the identified patient, sex of the therapist, socioeconomic status, religion, and race.

What would have been the results if IFI (*inpatient* family intervention) had been followed up with some outpatient family sessions? Future studies should assess the impact of "booster" outpatient sessions that build on a positive response to family work during the inpatient phase. It may be possible to differentiate between those families that need little or no postdischarge intervention and those that need further family intervention because of such factors as family denial of illness or long-standing conflict and lack of support for the patient. The next step in systematic research on IFI would be to test the incremental benefits of continuing such treatment into the post-hospitalization recovery phase.

REFERENCES

American Psychiatric Association: Diagnostic and Statistical Manual of Mental Disorders, 3rd Edition. Washington, DC, American Psychiatric Association, 1980

Biglan A, Hope H, Sherman L, et al: Problem-solving interactions of depressed women and their spouses. Behavioral Therapy (in press)

Billings AG, Moos R: Psychological stressors, coping, and depression, in Handbook of Depression: Treatment, Assessment, and Research. Edited by Beckham E, Leber W. Homewood, IL, Dorsey Press, 1985

Brown GW, Harris TO: Social Origins of Depression: A Study of Psychiatric Disorder in Women. New York, Free Press, 1978

Clarkin JF, Spencer JH, Peyser J, et al: IFI for psychotic disorders: a manual of inpatient family intervention. Unpublished manuscript, 1981

Coyne JC, Aldwin C, Lazarus RS: Depression and coping in stressful episodes. J Abnorm Psychol 90:439–447, 1981

Davenport YB, Adland ML: Family therapy intervention in the management of manic episodes, in Affective Disorders and Family Intervention. Edited by Clarkin JF, Haas G, Glick ID. New York, Guilford Press, 1988

Falloon IRH, Boyd JL, McGill CW, et al: Family management in the prevention of exacerbations of schizophrenia: a controlled study. N Engl J Med 306:1437–1440, 1982

Folkman S, Lazarus RS: Stress processes and depressive symptomatology. J Abnorm Psychol 95:107–113, 1986

Friedman AS: Interaction of drug therapy with marital therapy in depressive patients. Arch Gen Psychiatry 32:619–637, 1975

Glick ID, Clarkin JF, Spencer JH, et al: A controlled evaluation of inpatient family intervention. Arch Gen Psychiatry 42:882–886, 1985

Goldstein MJ, Rodnick EH, Evans JR, et al: Drug and family therapy in the affective treatment of acute schizophrenics. Arch Gen Psychiatry 35:1169–1177, 1978

Haas G, Clarkin JF, Glick ID: Marital and family treatment of depression, in Handbook of Depression: Treatment, Assessment, and Research. Edited by Beckham E, Leber W. Homewood, IL, Dorsey Press, 1985

Haas GL, Glick ID, Clarkin JF, et al: Inpatient family intervention: a controlled study, II: results at discharge. Arch Gen Psychiatry 45:217–224, 1988

Klerman GL, Weissman MM, Rounsaville BJ, et al: Interpersonal Psychotherapy of Depression. New York, Basic Books, 1984

Luborsky L, Crits-Christoph P, McLellan AT, et al: Do therapists vary much in their success? Findings from four outcome studies. Am J Orthopsychiatry 56:501–512, 1986

Rounsaville BJ, Weissman NW, Prusoff BA, et al: Marital disputes and treatment outcome in depressed women. Compr Psychiatry 20:483–490, 1979

Schaefer C, Coyne JC, Lazarus RS: The health-related functions of social support. J Behav Med 4:381–406, 1981

Wallace CJ, Liberman RP: Social skills training for patients with schizophrenia: a controlled clinical trial. Psychiatry Res 15:239–247, 1985

Weissman MM, Paykel E: The Depressed Woman: A Study of Social Relationships. Chicago, IL, University of Chicago Press, 1974

Wellisch DD, Vincent J, RoTrock G: Family therapy versus individual therapy: a study of adolescents and their parents, in Treating Relationships. Edited by Olson D. Lake Mills, IA, Graphic Publishing Co, 1976

Chapter 7

Social Learning–Based Marital Therapy and Cognitive Therapy as a Combined Treatment for Depression

Sandra J. Coffman, Ph.D.
Neil S. Jacobson, Ph.D.

Chapter 7

Social Learning–Based Marital Therapy and Cognitive Therapy as a Combined Treatment for Depression

The importance of developing an effective treatment for depression is illustrated by the estimate that 25% of the general population will experience at least one debilitating affective episode in their lifetime (Weissman et al. 1978). Until recently, depressive disorders have primarily been treated individually. Several treatment approaches, including psychotherapy and psychopharmacotherapy, have provided evidence of their efficacy in treating depression (Bellack et al. 1983; Kovacs 1980; Kovacs et al. 1981; Steinbrueck et al. 1983; Weissman et al. 1979).

However, not everyone responds to these individual treatments. Even for those who do respond initially, recurrences are common (Rush et al. 1977). This realization, as well as the influence of feminist and systems theorists (e.g., Hare-Muston 1978), has led to a recent and growing appreciation by researchers of the interpersonal aspects of depression (Brown and Harris 1978; Coyne and Gotlib 1985; Coyne 1976; Coyne et al. 1987; Gotlib 1982; Gotlib and Colby, in press; Gotlib and Hooley, in press; Hooley 1986; Hooley et al. 1986). The marital relationship has been one focus of this attention.

Researchers are beginning to investigate the role of close relationships in the cause and treatment of depression, as well as the negative impact of depression on close relationships. In addition, researchers and clinicians are also examining the importance of involving family members in the actual therapy process with the depressed client (Beach and O'Leary 1986; Coyne 1984; Dobson et al., in press; Follette and Jacobson, in press; Jacobson 1984; Rounsaville et al. 1983).

Marriage seems to offer some protection against depression for men but generally not for women (Weissman and Klerman 1977). In fact, married women are particularly at risk for depression in comparison with unmarried women (Overall 1971). Renne (1971) and Ilfield (1977) also provided evidence of the link between marital distress and depression for both men and women. Therefore, clinical interventions that improve the marital relationship might reduce both initial incidences and recurrences of depression. In fact, studies have suggested that the prognosis for sustained reduction of depression is poorer if marital conflict exists (Klerman and Weissman 1982; Rounsaville and Chevron 1982). Finally, the argument for combining treatments for marital distress and depression flows from the fact that the two phenomena often appear to occur simultaneously (Beach et al. 1985; Feldman 1976; Rounsaville et al. 1979).

This chapter presents a rationale, model, and case history combining social learning–based marital therapy (Jacobson and Holtzworth-Munroe 1986; Jacobson and Margolin 1979) with individual cognitive-behavior therapy for depression (Beck et al. 1979). Cognitive therapy was chosen because of its widely reported efficacy in treating depression (Beck et al. 1985; Kovacs 1980; Rush et al. 1977, 1982; Shaw 1977). By contrast, only a few studies have directly evaluated marital therapy as a treatment for depression, although it is sometimes used to treat interpersonal relationships in which one partner is depressed. Interpersonal therapy, until now, has only reported data with the depressed spouse as the client (Klerman and Weissman 1982; Rounsaville and Chevron 1982). However, marital therapy has a very poor success rate when not conducted conjointly (Gurman and Kniskern 1981). One form of conjointly structured marital therapy, social learning–based marital therapy, has continued to test and expand its focus by including cognitive interventions (Jacobson and Holtzworth-Munroe 1986). Because cognitive therapy and social learning–based marital therapy rest on similar theoretical frameworks, they are compatible. Both are also designed as short-term therapies and present to clients a philosophy-based collaborative empiricism. At times, this integrated form of therapy provides a more comprehensive treatment program for depressed people in general, particularly for women.

DESCRIPTION OF THE MODEL

This treatment was developed as part of a research study sponsored by the National Institute of Mental Health. This time-limited treatment consisted of 20 sessions that could be divided as clinically indicated between individual cognitive-behavior therapy (Beck et al.

1979) for the depressed woman and conjoint social learning–based marital therapy (Jacobson and Margolin 1979; Jacobson and Holtzworth-Munroe 1986) for her and her partner. Different combinations of individual cognitive and marital therapy were used depending on the needs of each couple. However, a minimum of 12 cognitive sessions plus 8 marital sessions were required in the research study. In a few cases, the 20-session limit was varied due to extreme clinical considerations.

The first 2 weeks of treatment always included four sessions of individual cognitive therapy to begin to address the woman's depression and one joint session with the couple. If possible, the husband was also interviewed individually (as part of marital therapy) in the first 2 weeks. The third marital session followed the roundtable format (Jacobson and Holtzworth-Munroe 1986) to present both partners with an outline of marital therapy designed for their particular needs and to ask them to commit to the hard work of therapy as outlined. However, by this time, the woman was typically quite engaged and committed to individual cognitive therapy. Thus, the choice of the couple to not engage in the marital therapy was made considerably less often than in traditional marital therapy. Instead, the husbands often gave grudging consent to marital therapy in order to allow their wives to continue individual therapy. This is clearly a less than ideal beginning for couples work but a not uncommon problem in clinical practice, because the woman often initiates treatment.

Our rationale for generally beginning therapy with cognitive sessions is multifaceted. The initial individual sessions present a cognitive model of depression and describe the process of cognitive therapy. We ask the client to read a small pamphlet titled "Coping With Depression" (Beck and Greenberg 1974) between the first and second sessions. The first homework assignment is to monitor her behavior and mood on an hourly basis. The client's reactions to this assignment and to the pamphlet often predict how favorably she will respond to cognitive therapy. This information can then be included in treatment decisions, including the frequency and overall scheduling of marital sessions. Early cognitive sessions also allow us to monitor and treat any indications of potential for suicide.

Clients typically experienced great relief at beginning a therapy that so immediately and directly addressed their depressive symptoms. Many clients' depression lifted immediately and significantly in these early sessions. As the woman became less depressed, she sometimes blamed herself less for marital dissatisfaction and became angry at her partner, causing the treatment emphasis to shift to marital work. (For a case example of this dynamic, see Dobson et al., in press.)

In other cases, as the woman became less depressed, she became more aware of the love and support her partner had been trying to offer her. Partners of depressed clients often become discouraged when their attempts to provide help are ignored or misinterpreted, which can result from the depressed person's selective negative focus. In this case, both partners will often be more collaborative and hopeful when the woman's depression has lifted somewhat, making this a more fruitful time to begin marital therapy. This benefit must, of course, be balanced against the following dangers of beginning with individual therapy: 1) seeming to identify the depressed person as the identified patient and 2) the possibility that the husband will feel excluded or alienated as a result of the therapeutic alliance between the therapist and his partner.

In our work, we identified four types of depressive marital constellations (Dobson et al., in press), each of which interacted differently with our combined treatment, leading to some structural differences in the treatment.

Classic couples present with complaints of both depression and marital distress. These couples seemed most ideally suited for the combined treatment, wherein the two component treatments often had an interactive and synergistic effect. Therefore, a treatment plan would often involve approximately a 50-50 split between individual and marital therapy. The case presented later in this chapter illustrates the use of the combined treatment in a classic couple.

Denial couples identify the wife as depressed but both deny marital problems. Yet our marital assessment identifies them as distressed. Consequently, at least one partner often reacts negatively to the suggestion that the relationship requires conjoint therapy, so these couples can be difficult to treat. However, because the likelihood of relapse is high if the marital relationship is not improved, the combined treatment can be quite beneficial. To engage these couples in therapy, early sessions focus on cognitive therapy augmented by some contact with the nondepressed partner. The spouse is asked to participate as a resource for the depressed partner and is given support and empathy for the difficulty in living with a depressed person.

If the marital distress is actually a reaction to depression, the marriage may spontaneously improve to some degree as the woman's depression lifts from individual therapy. Marital therapy can then focus on strengthening and enhancing the marriage. If, however, marital problems underlie depression, the early cognitive sessions often illuminate this as self-criticism on the part of the depressed spouse diminishes. More anger is then directed toward the nondepressed partner, provoking a minor crisis within the marriage. The problem of denial is now diminished at least by half, and marital therapy can help the couple begin necessary changes in their relationship. If the couple were not in combined treatment, it is more likely that this crisis could lead to separation and/or divorce. This may be a healthy and necessary course of action even with combined treatment, but if both partners wish instead to change the marriage, the combined treatment provides them a ready opportunity to do so.

Systemic couples present complaining only of marital problems, but careful assessment convinces the therapist that one or both partners suffer from major depression. Although both agree to the need for marital therapy, they may object to the adjunct use of individual cognitive sessions, which are particularly useful if depression originally triggered marital distress. Cognitive therapy is less likely to be necessary or useful if the marital discord precipitated the depression because improvement in the marriage via marital therapy may itself result in a reduction in depression.

Finally, *social support* couples acknowledge that one partner is depressed, but they deny marital distress, which is also found to be absent after a careful marital assessment. Because the relationship has remained strong, the treatment plan should focus on individual cognitive therapy, but some marital sessions may enhance the social support for the depressed spouse. Because the depression of one spouse almost always reduces time and attention given to the relationship, behavior exchange procedures can help the couple focus again on each other and diminish their preoccupation with depression. When clinical depression develops, parenting, household tasks, financial responsibilities, joint social time, and pleasurable sexual relationships are often disrupted. Problem-solving training and attention to rebuilding affectionate and sexual relationships can provide a safe and effective format for dealing with the resultant problems.

In summary, this combination treatment provides a flexible approach to dealing with various kinds of responses to the interaction of depression and marital problems in various kinds of couples. Classic couples tended to receive a 50-50 split in individual and marital therapy throughout their sessions, whereas denial and social support couples focused more heavily on individual therapy, and systemic couples were treated more heavily with marital therapy in the early part of therapy. The latter half of therapy varied more, both according to couple typology and individual couple needs.

ADVANTAGES AND DIFFICULTIES FOR THE THERAPIST

The advantages of combined treatment include

1. The ability to see the marital system at work and, therefore, the opportunity to help change dysfunctional interactions;
2. Access to cognitions and behavior of both partners, as well as to observing how these both interact;
3. The ability to support the couple in making necessary healthy changes if the depressed wife gets angry as she becomes less depressed; and
4. Theoretical compatibility for conceptualizing the case, because there is much similarity between the underpinnings of both treatment modalities.

There are also, however, theoretical contradictions and clinical disadvantages in combining individual cognitive and marital therapy:

1. A strong, separate alliance may develop between the therapist and the depressed spouse, due to their individual sessions.
2. The individual cognitive sessions may imply that the depressed client is the identified patient and that the depression has a cause apart from the marriage (which may or may not be true), thereby diminishing the marital therapy assumption of reciprocal responsibility.
3. Confusion may result from the very different approaches to incomplete homework. (See Beck et al. 1979 and Jacobson and Holtzworth-Munroe 1986 for these opposing strategies.)
4. Only the depressed partner can get cognitive training, although the therapist can explore the thinking of the nondepressed spouse in the marital sessions.
5. The therapist may experience role confusion, feeling unsure whether he or she is the couple's or the depressed partner's therapist.

In addition, certain difficulties were either inherent in or heightened by the constraints of our short-term therapy model: 1) The limit of 20 sessions (of 1–1.5 hours maximum) meant that sometimes both treatment modalities got short shrift and neither had a real trial. 2) Many couples have multiple individual and marital issues, which cannot all be resolved in 20 sessions despite their heightened expectations for themselves and their mates, with the possible negative outcome of discouraging them from future therapy. (Is a little bit of two kinds of therapy a dangerous thing?) 3) Neither therapy includes a format for interviewing or including children, even adolescents, in therapy although many marital issues focus on parenting. 4) We relied on self-report for marital violence and alcohol abuse and other problem behaviors (such as gambling) despite people's tendency to minimize these issues and our inability to treat them effectively within this time-constrained model. Careful assessment of these issues should *always* precede the decision to work conjointly with a couple so as not to minimize their effects on depression or especially not to further endanger a woman's life. Marital therapy can exacerbate marital violence. (For further discussion of these issues, see NiCarthy et al. 1984.)

Some of the advantages and disadvantages of this integrated model are highlighted in the following case history.

CASE HISTORY

Gwen, age 41, and Keith, age 36, a systemic couple, entered therapy because of Gwen's depression of several months duration. Her pretest score on the Beck Depression Inventory (BDI) was 21, and she scored 15 on the Hamilton Rating Scale for Depression. She reported both somatic and cognitive symptoms of depression. Self-criticism and disappointment in herself were cognitive themes associated with her depression. She met DSM-III criteria for major affective disorder, recurrent.

Although Gwen had experienced depression at other stressful points in her life, beginning with adolescence, both Keith and Gwen agreed this episode of depression began immediately after Keith had revealed he had lost a great deal of their joint money through gambling. Gwen felt especially betrayed and humiliated because he had previously lied to her when she questioned him about discrepancies in their finances.

Because of our short-term model, Keith and Gwen were immediately informed by their therapist that we would not have time to deal directly with Keith's problem with gambling. Keith was willing to make a no-gambling contract for the duration of therapy, something he had never tried before. This contract was defined and clarified over several sessions to include every conceivable situation of profit for chance, including baseball pools, computer games, and penny card games. Once these stipulations were clarified, Keith was able to keep to the contract, much to Gwen's surprise and relief. She interpreted this effort as evidence of his caring for her, creating hope and slowly rebuilding trust. However, had Keith been unwilling to attempt this contract (or had he failed at it), he would have been referred to Gamblers Anonymous and possibly individual behavior therapy for gambling.

Gwen disliked the role of interrogator and instigator of most of their social interactions. Both were successful in their professional careers. Keith, a small-businessperson, had great difficulty limiting his time at work, consequently reducing his time with Gwen. He also used his work (and subsequent fatigue) as an excuse to avoid resolving conflictual interactions with Gwen. His lying had partially been an attempt to avoid conflict with Gwen, as well as representing a serious denial of the gravity of his financial difficulties.

Keith is a second-generation Filipino, the middle of three children. His parents and grandparents worked very hard at their family business. Although his family did not express caring directly, he had the feeling of being loved but wanted more approval. His mother would scream and yell when upset, and his father would withdraw, a pattern repeated in Keith and Gwen's marriage. For as long as he could remember, gambling was an accepted part of his family of origin's social life.

Keith worked very hard in college and experienced his father's approval shortly before his father's death. At age 23, he began living with Gwen and her two children, but she "threw him out" when he dated another woman. This caused him to reevaluate his commitment, and 6 months later after Gwen proposed, they married.

Gwen was from an emotionally very expressive Italian family. Conflict was open and frequent. She maintained relatively close contact with her mother, although throughout her life she had felt her mother was extremely critical of her. Gwen also feared she was becoming overly critical of Keith, as she viewed her mother as having been with her deceased father. Gwen's oldest brother had always been extremely critical of her weight, even though she viewed herself as "sturdy, not fat" as a child and adolescent. When Gwen was a teenager, her mother joined him in this critical refrain. Gwen quickly learned to joke about her weight and to laugh at herself before others did, as a defense against their criticism.

Another painful memory involved her mother's return to work when Gwen was 9 years old. Left alone from 3:00 to 6:00 P.M., she felt extremely lonely, and eating became a solace. Late into therapy, she tied this experience to a lifelong assumption that "If people love me, they'll want to be with me" and its corollary "If people are absent or late, it means they don't care about me." She also began to see how she had learned to use food as comfort.

Gwen married for the first time at age 18, when she was pregnant. She dropped out of college and raised two children. She had a great deal of difficulty losing weight after each pregnancy and gradually gained weight. Her husband drank excessively, was verbally abusive, and was especially critical of her weight gain, calling her a fat pig. She divorced him when she discovered he was having an affair. She subsequently married a man 10 years her senior, with whom she remains close friends. But he was impatient with her children, and they drifted apart because he worked evenings. He initially encouraged her friendship with Keith, with whom she worked.

At intake, Gwen and Keith had been married for 10 years. He indicated great commitment to the marriage and a desire to win back her trust and to "have peace in the family." He was willing to stop gambling. Gwen, however, had considered separation and was unsure if she could rebuild her trust in Keith. Both had enjoyed raising Gwen's children, one of whom was now in college and one planning to leave for college in 6 months. They both expressed sadness and excitement at the opportunity to be a couple living alone for the first time in their relationship. Both Gwen and Keith acknowledged cultural and stylistic differences in themselves but found these differences more exciting than negative.

Because Keith and Gwen both acknowledged the impact of marital issues and distrust on Gwen's depression, marital therapy was immediately begun in conjunction with individual cognitive sessions. The couple sessions began with teaching positive behavior exchange. Both partners responded immediately and creatively to this task, developing numerous ways to express caring for the other, including the following: they left greeting cards in each other's car; she put toothpaste on a toothbrush and left it out for him when he was turning in late; he left her a love note on a mirror; she made him rice—his favorite food—every night for a week; and he surprised her at work on their anniversary and took her out to lunch.

Gwen and Keith also welcomed the chance to spend more social time together, since they had fallen into a rut of spending each Saturday evening with the same couple, often gambling for spare change. When this was ruled out due to Keith's "no-gambling contract," they rediscovered old social pleasures and developed new ones. Alternate weeks, each was assigned the homework of inviting the other on a special date. Both put an unusual amount of time and effort into designing original dates that their partner would enjoy. We praised them and emphasized that this effort represented a commitment to enriching their life together as a couple. We also stressed that this was especially important at this time when their last child was leaving home.

The combination of positive behavior change and increased pleasurable social time, along with their relief at being in therapy and the no-gambling control, quickly brought hope and energy to this marriage. This optimism prepared them to continue the hard work of therapy, which then proceeded with communication and problem-solving training, which will later be described in detail.

Meanwhile, Gwen's individual sessions of cognitive-behavior therapy focused on increasing behavior that provided her with feelings of competency and pleasure, as well as on increasing her social contacts. For example, instead of waiting alone for Keith to return home from work, she was encouraged to visit with or to telephone friends. Because she was critical of herself for watching television, she began to instead read a book for 1 hour a week.

We then began tracking her automatic thoughts, using the Dysfunctional Thought Log. For several weeks, she simply recorded thoughts, accompanying feelings, and precipitating situations in the first three columns. Then she began attempting more realistic replies to distorted thoughts and recording any subsequent shift in her feelings in the fourth and fifth columns. Gwen was relieved to be able to see a connection between her thoughts and feelings and was pleased to be able to affect her moods. She became less depressed and more hopeful both about decreasing her depression and about rekindling her marriage. Her score on the BDI fell to an 8 on the 7th session and only rose above 8 during two relapses in the 14th and 17th sessions, both associated with thoughts about her weight.

Some of Gwen's automatic thoughts dealt with her desire for more attention and time from her youngest daughter and from her husband. She also examined negative predictions about her daughters deserting her permanently after they left home, fearing they would choose to spend much more time with her ex-husband, due to his wealth. She was relieved that discussions with her daughters and examination of their past behavior provided no real evidence of this extreme prediction. Instead, she began to view her daughters' physical separation from her as a healthy step in their process of maturation and individuation.

Automatic thoughts also revealed a high need for attention and high standards for herself that were currently unmet. In the ninth session, she said, "I'm not the success I've been in the past. I'm not the star. I'm only in the chorus line, and it's not good enough." Gwen actually had sung with a band as a teenager and had felt like a star. Her father had been in professional sports. Therefore, we explored the possibility of her finding ways to feel more in the limelight (changing the situation) while we also examined the effect on her mood of these kinds of expectations (changing cognitions).

The couple sessions at the midpoint of therapy focused on searching and practicing reflective listening and on making "I" statements.

Gwen felt great relief at being truly listened to, as opposed to Keith's pattern of withdrawing from either direct expression of feelings or from conflict. Keith was relieved that Gwen's feelings were increasingly positive. He also found she needed less attention overall if he provided some direct, genuine communication, instead of half listening or pretending everything was always just fine. For example, once he heard Gwen's reactions of hurt and rejection when he was late, they were able to jointly approach this problem. We also worked on Gwen's feelings of rejection in her individual cognitive sessions.

Keith's fear of direct conflict was also lessened by the very structured format for problem solving, which we began in the 13th session. Often the combined treatment does not allow for formal problem-solving training, but this couple worked quickly and collaboratively. Their sexual relationship continued to be good, so no therapy time was needed for that important issue. Because both responded very favorably to reading our problem-solving manual, we decided to use the last part of therapy for conflict resolution using written change agreements. (For further discussion, see Jacobson and Margolin 1979 and Jacobson and Holtzworth-Munroe 1986.) Both were relieved when they jointly resolved conflict about lateness, driving in the car together, cooking, and other household chores. They also contracted to deal in very particular ways with a future social engagement where many people gambled.

Meanwhile, the individual therapy explored Gwen's automatic thoughts and underlying beliefs and assumptions. As previously mentioned, Keith's lateness resulted in her thinking, "Everyone should always be perfectly on time if they care at all about me" (an impossible standard), about which she could eventually laugh. Its corollary was explored, "If they're ever at all late, they don't care about me," and Gwen developed a list of other ways she and others expressed caring (including some of the behavior exchange examples previously discussed). Ways of making her social and work life more exciting were explored, as well as her desire to be a star. Many "shoulds" were examined for their utility, in view of the great guilt they caused her. Empathy and humor aided our efforts in this more exploratory part of therapy.

In individual sessions, we touched on Gwen's fears of losing her daughters and her feeling of loss when her first husband was unfaithful. Then, in the 16th session, this dynamic was evident in the couples session as the lateness issue once again reared its head, illuminating their dance about intimacy. The steps seemed to be as follows:

1. Gwen brings up a conflict.
2. Keith is scared, so sidesteps and withdraws.
3. Gwen feels alone and abandoned or gets angry.
4. Keith feels guilty in either case and withdraws further, and so on.

The couple subsequently identified examples of this dance themselves and were able to identify it or to stop it at the time because each recognized it brought them the opposite of what they wanted. Keith, the peace seeker, ended up with a sobbing or enraged spouse (just like his mother), whereas Gwen, who sought contact and problem solution, had alienated and distanced Keith. Because they both acknowledged their own role in this dance, they were able to propose and act out alternative steps that got them more of what they wanted.

The couple was very much reconnected and trust was almost rebuilt by the 17th session. They began to plan for ending therapy by beginning weekly "state of the relationship" meetings (Jacobson and Holtzworth-Munroe 1986) to check on each other and to anticipate any future problems. Plans were also made for how they would proceed if there was relapse in Keith's gambling, including the possibility of Gamblers Anonymous or individual psychotherapy.

Previously, Gwen had experienced a relapse of depression in the 14th session. This was precipitated in a small degree by Keith's refusal to accept her despair about not losing weight, even though on a weight-reduction program. I reiterated the importance of each person being seen as the expert on their own feelings, whereas the opposite partner's job initially was to try to understand them fully—a return to active listening skills.

In our individual session, Gwen rephrased this for herself as, "There is no 'should' about feelings; they just are." This also enabled her to reduce her self-criticism about her own reaction to her weight gain and to more fully explore her own thoughts and feelings and their depressing effect on her mood.

Early in therapy, Gwen had decided to return to a very structured diet program that had worked quickly for her in the past. I expressed my concern about the yo-yo effect of diets, but she proceeded. This time, however, she lost weight much more slowly. This realization precipitated the thought that "No one will love me if I'm this fat." Gwen weighed around 200 pounds, was in excellent health, and was extremely attractive to many people. In fact, when (as a homework assignment) she checked with her daughter, her husband, and several friends, they all assured her of their continuing love for her and of their acceptance of her appearance. This had a very powerful effect; her BDI score dropped from a 26 to a 5 by the next session.

She subsequently decided to stop trying to lose weight on such a restrictive diet and began a structured maintenance program. However, in our 19th session, her BDI score shot up again to a 17 after she gained 5 pounds. This was also several days before her youngest daughter's departure for college and 2 weeks before the termination of therapy.

Gwen asked for an extension of therapy, which was granted on clinical grounds. Because the marital progress was not shaken at all by this relapse, marital therapy finished on schedule, with both partners feeling optimistic about their skills and progress. Gwen's BDI score was 12 at the 20th session.

Two additional individual sessions of cognitive therapy resulted in a gradual reduction of BDI scores to a 9 and then a 3. Issues explored cognitively included separation issues, body image, and self-worth, including Gwen's statement, "I hate myself," although she realized others loved her. She explored the extreme medical interventions of stomach stapling and ballooning but decided—to our great relief—to instead design her own health program. This included joining a gym for daily workouts (to augment daily walks), eating in a healthy way, and monitoring her cognitive and situational cues for snacking. She also bought herself some attractive new clothes and asked her husband to give her compliments on her body and appearance when he could. She told friends she was not dieting any more and asked them to help explore more exciting career possibilities. She discovered she often snacked when bored or wanting comfort, especially at times when she would have sucked her thumb as a child.

Obviously, therapy could have continued further at this point. However, she felt ready to stop, armed with some suggestions for reading. She felt she could better predict and interrupt future relapses and felt good about both the individual and marital therapy. Because her BDI score (Beck et al. 1979) dropped to a 3, I concurred, and therapy was terminated, as planned, after this 22nd session. Follow-up data 1 year later revealed a continued cessation of depression, with a BDI score of 0. (Her husband's BDI was 1). Both husband's and wife's scores at 1-year follow-up also indicated an absence of marital distress; her score on the Dyadic Adjustment Scale (Spanier 1976) was 121 and his was 133, and both obtained global distress scores on the Marital Satisfaction Inventory (Snyder 1979) of 42.

CONCLUSIONS

This case illustrates the synergistic effects of combining individual cognitive therapy for a depressed woman with marital therapy for her and her partner.

Our initial research has highlighted both advantages and disadvantages of this new combined treatment for depression and marital difficulties that result from and/or cause the wife's depression. Further research and clinical experience are now necessary to identify ways to minimize the difficulties and to maximize the advantages of this model. As therapists in private practice and in agencies apply this model without research constraints, information about its use in more flexible settings will become available and, in turn, influence subsequent research.

REFERENCES

American Psychiatric Association: Diagnostic and Statistical Manual of Mental Disorders, 3rd Edition. Washington, DC, American Psychiatric Association, 1980

Beach SRH, O'Leary KD: The treatment of depression occurring in the context of marital discord. Behavioral Therapy 17:43–49, 1986

Beach SRH, Jouriles EN, O'Leary KD: Extramarital sex: impact on depression and commitment in couples seeking marital therapy. J Sex Marital Ther 11:99–108, 1985

Beck AT, Greenberg R: Coping With Depression. New York, Institute for Rational Living, 1974

Beck AT, Rush AJ, Shaw B, et al: Cognitive Therapy of Depression. New York, Guilford Press, 1979

Beck AT, Hollon SD, Young JE, et al: Treatment of depression with cognitive therapy and amitriptyline. Arch Gen Psychiatry 42:142–148, 1985

Bellack AS, Hersen M, Himmelhoch JM: A comparison of social-skills training, pharmacotherapy and psychotherapy for depression. Behav Res Ther 21:101–107, 1983

Brown GW, Harris T: Social Origins of Depression. New York, Free Press, 1978

Coyne JC: Toward an interactional description of depression. Psychiatry 39:28–40, 1976

Coyne JC: Strategic therapy with married depressed persons: initial agenda, themes, and interventions. Journal of Marital and Family Therapy 10:53–62, 1984

Coyne JC, Gotlib IH: Implicit theories of psychopathology: implications for interpersonal conceptualizations of depression. Social Cognition 3:341–368, 1985

Coyne JC, Kahn J, Gotlib IH: Depression, in Family Interaction and Psychopathology. Edited by Jacob T. New York, Plenum Press, 1987

Dobson KS, Jacobson NS, Victor J: Towards an integration of cognitive therapy and behavioral marital therapy for depression, in Family Variables in Intervention in Affective Illness. Edited by Clarkin JF, Haas G, Glick I. New York, Guilford Press, 1988

Feldman LB: Depression and marital interaction. Fam Process 15:389–395, 1976

Follette WC, Jacobson NS: Behavioral marital therapy in the treatment of depressive disorders, in Handbook of Behavioral Family Therapy. Edited by Falloon IRH. New York, Guilford Press, 1988

Gotlib IH: Self-reinforcement and depression in interpersonal interaction: the role of performance level. J Abnorm Psychol 91:3–13, 1982

Gotlib IH, Colby CA: Treatment of Depression: An Interpersonal Systems Approach. New York, Pergamon Press, 1987

Gotlib IH, Hooley JM: Depression and marital distress, in Handbook of Personal Relationships. Edited by Duck S. New York, Wiley, 1988

Gurman AS, Kniskern DP: Family therapy outcome research: knowns and unknowns, in Handbook of Family Therapy. Edited by Gurman AS, Kniskern DP. New York, Brunner/Mazel, 1981

Hare-Muston RT: A feminist approach to family therapy. Fam Process 17:181–194, 1978

Hooley JM: Expressed emotion and depression: interactions between patients and high- versus low-expressed emotion spouses. J Abnorm Psychol 95:237–276, 1986

Hooley JM, Orley J, Teasdale JD: Levels of expressed emotion and relapse in depressed patients. Br J Psychiatry 148:642–647, 1986

Ilfield FW: Current social stressors and symptoms of depression. Am J Psychiatry 134:161–166, 1977

Jacobson NS: Marital therapy and the cognitive-behavioral treatment of depression. The Behavior Therapist 7:143–147, 1984

Jacobson NS, Holtzworth-Munroe A: Marital therapy: a social learning-cognitive perspective, in Clinical Handbook of Marital Therapy. Edited by Jacobson NS, Gurman AS. New York, Guilford Press, 1986

Jacobson NS, Margolin G: Marital Therapy: Strategies Based on Social Learning and Behavior Exchange Principles. New York, Brunner/Mazel, 1979

Klerman GL, Weissman MM: Interpersonal psychotherapy: theory and research, in Short-Term Psychotherapies for Depression. Edited by Rush AJ. New York, Guilford Press, 1982

Kovacs M: The efficacy of cognitive and behavioral therapies for depression. Am J Psychiatry 137:1495–1504, 1980

Kovacs M, Rush AJ, Beck AT, et al: Depressed outpatients treated with cognitive therapy or pharmacotherapy. Arch Gen Psychiatry 38:33–39, 1981

NiCarthy G, Merriam K, Coffman S: Talking It Out: Groups for Abused Women. Seattle, Seal Press, 1984

Overall J: Associations between marital history and the nature of manifest psychopathology. J Abnorm Psychol 78:213–221, 1971

Renne KS: Health and marital experience in an urban population. Journal of Marriage and the Family 33:338–350, 1971

Rounsaville BJ, Chevron E: Interpersonal psychotherapy: clinical applications, in Short-Term Psychotherapies for Depression. Edited by Rush AJ. New York, Guilford Press, 1982

Rounsaville BJ, Weissman MM, Prusoff BS, et al: Marital disputes and treatment outcome in depressed women. Compr Psychiatry 20:483–490, 1979

Rounsaville BJ, Klerman GL, Weissman MM, et al: Interpersonal psychotherapy for depression: conjoint marital. Unpublished treatment manual, Massachusetts General Hospital, Boston, 1983

Rush AJ, Beck AT, Kovacs M, et al: Comparative efficacy of cognitive therapy and imipramine in the treatment of depressed outpatients. Cognitive Therapy and Research 1:17–37, 1977

Rush AJ, Beck AT, Weissenburger J, et al: Comparison of the effects of cognitive therapy and pharmacotherapy on hopelessness and self-concept. Am J Psychiatry 139:862–866, 1982

Shaw B: A comparison of cognitive therapy and behavior therapy in the treatment of depression. J Consult Clin Psychol 45:543–551, 1977

Snyder DK: Multidimensional assessment of marital satisfaction. Journal of Marriage and the Family 41:813–823, 1979

Spanier GB: Measuring dyadic adjustment: new scales for assessing the quality of marriage and similar dyads. Journal of Marriage and the Family 38:15–28, 1976

Steinbrueck SM, Maxwell DE, Howard GS: A meta-analysis of psychotherapy and drug therapy in the treatment of unipolar depression with adults. J Consult Clin Psychol 51:856–863, 1983

Weissman MM, Klerman GL: Sex differences in the epidemiology of depression. Arch Gen Psychiatry 34:98–111, 1977

Weissman MM, Myers JK, Hardey PS: Psychiatric disorders in a U.S. urban community: 1975–1976. Am J Psychiatry 135:459–462, 1978

Weissman MM, Prusoff BA, DiMascio A, et al: The efficacy of drugs and psychotherapy in the treatment of acute depression. Am J Psychiatry 136:555–558, 1979

Chapter 8

Psychoeducational Family Intervention for Depressed Patients and Their Families

Diane Holder, M.S.W.
Carol Anderson, Ph.D.

Chapter 8

Psychoeducational Family Intervention for Depressed Patients and Their Families

Described in ancient Greece as melancholia or "black bile," depressive disorders have been visible over the centuries and today remain the most prevalent form of mental illness. Although depression occurs in varying forms and degrees, the point prevalence for nonbipolar depression in industrialized countries is estimated at 3% for men and 4–9% for women. This translates into a lifetime risk between 8 and 12% for men and 20 and 26% for women (Boyd and Weissman 1981). Fortunately, there is early evidence from controlled studies that both pharmacologic and individually oriented psychological interventions can be effective in the treatment of acute episodes as well as in the prevention of relapse (Beck et al. 1979; Elkin et al. 1986; Klerman et al. 1984; Rush et al. 1977; Shaw 1977; Weissman 1979). The role of the family in the treatment process, however, has received less attention. Despite numerous studies identifying family and marital problems in depressed patients (Coyne 1976; Hinchliffe et al. 1975; Rounsaville et al. 1980; Weissman and Paykel 1974), systematic interventions designed specifically for families with a depressed member have only begun to be developed (Birchler 1986; Coyne 1984, 1986; Jacobson 1984a; Papolos 1984). This chapter describes one such effort, a psychoeducational treatment approach designed to help these families and patients understand and cope with serious and/or recurrent depressive illness.

Psychoeducational family therapy was originally developed as part of a larger research project involving schizophrenic patients and their families (Anderson et al. 1980, 1986b). Data from this project (Hogarty et al. 1986, 1987) and other similar programs with a family education component (Goldstein and Kopeikin 1981; Falloon et al. 1982; Leff and Vaughn 1981) suggest that these therapeutic interventions, combined with a medication program, can influence the course of chronic mental disorders by postponing relapse and averting crises. More recently, similar approaches have begun to be applied to persons experiencing affective disorders (Anderson and Reiss 1984; Anderson et al. 1986b; Papolos 1984).

The rationale for the use of a psychoeducational model with serious depression is based on several hypotheses: that both biological and interpersonal factors play a role in the onset and course of depression; that families are a valuable resource for effectively managing the disorder; and that information and support can decrease stress for both the patient and the family. Although no controlled studies to date verify the effectiveness of a psychoeducational model with this population, the likelihood that past and current interpersonal stressors increase an individual's vulnerability to depression and the likelihood that distressed relationships will develop secondary to depressive episodes invite family intervention.

DESCRIPTION AND BASIC ASSUMPTION

The basic format of the proposed treatment is similar to the program designed by one of the authors (C.A.) for schizophrenia. It includes three stages: 1) connecting with the family, 2) providing information and coping skills, and 3) facilitating the application and maintenance of this information in everyday life. This chapter will describe the underlying assumptions of this proposed treatment, its goals, and the three phases of treatment. It will conclude with a section on the modifications necessary to apply the model to various age groupings. The proposed intervention includes a set of basic psychoeducational principles that have been adapted to apply specifically to depressive illness. These basic principles include

1. *Genetic and/or biological vulnerability are contributing factors in the development of depressive disorders.*

There are several lines of research suggesting that depression is a familial disorder and that genetic and/or biochemical variables play a pathogenic role in the development of a depressive disorder (Papolos and Papolos 1987). Investigators are exploring various avenues in an attempt to understand why depression appears in specific families, particularly to sort out the possible contributions of biochemical and genetic factors.

Current research has focused on several distinct but related areas: family aggregation studies that demonstrate that relatives of depressed patients have a significantly higher rate of affective illness than normal controls (Winokur et al. 1978; Weissman and Akiskal

1984), genetic linkage studies that attempt to find biological markers by examining family pedigrees of affectively loaded families (Kidd et al. 1984), twin studies that indicate findings such as significantly higher concordance rates for unipolar depression in monozygotic twins than in dizygotic twins (Bertelsen et al. 1977; Schlesser and Altshuler 1983), and adoption studies that try to further ferret out the role of heredity versus environment by contrasting twins reared apart or by comparing adopted children with their biological and adoptive families (Schlesser and Altshuler 1983). Additionally, biochemical studies are proceeding, including research related to neurotransmitter studies (Post and Ballenger 1984), physiological stress-response studies (Anisman and Zacharko 1982), neuroendocrine studies (Carroll et al. 1981), sleep studies (Kupfer et al. 1983), and studies of pharmacologic treatments (Charney and Menker 1981). These genetic and biological variables are hypothesized as relevant in the etiology and/or maintenance of depressive disorders, but the full extent of their influence remains speculative.

2. *Family variables are relevant in depression.*

Most family-oriented clinicians believe that early family experiences such as loss, abuse, and neglect may contribute to later psychological vulnerability, and current relationships influence and are influenced by depression. Numerous studies demonstrate a correlation between family variables and onset, course, and treatment outcome of depression. Although no controlled studies confirm a role for these variables in the etiology of depression, several family and interactional variables are of interest. Recent work indicates that the symptoms experienced by depressed individuals (i.e., sad affect, negative cognitions, isolative or agitated behavior) appear to have a clear impact on those who interact with them (Coyne et al. 1987). Ratings after a brief telephone contact with a depressed person suggest a negative impact on the reported mood of the nondepressed listener (Coyne 1976; Hammen and Peters 1978). Other studies indicate that during an acute episode, depressed mothers are less involved with their children and demonstrate more negative affect (Weissman 1972). These children, in turn, appear to be at increased risk for psychological problems and accidents (Brown et al. 1972; Beardslee et al. 1983), and both the children and spouses of depressed patients have been reported to make more visits to their family doctor (Widmer et al. 1980).

Current family, and especially marital, problems frequently are cited as correlates of depression (Merikangas et al. 1985). Some reports identify depression as an antecedent of marital discord (Briscoe and Smith 1973), whereas others report dysfunction in the marital relationship both before and after the acute episode of depression (Weissman 1979). Factors that have been cited as possibly contributing to reports of marital unhappiness include the alleged dominance by husbands of depressed wives (Hooley et al. 1986; Collins et al. 1971), a lack of intimacy and autonomy (Weissman and Paykel 1974), struggles for control or coercive interaction (Seligman et al. 1979; McLean and Hakistan 1979), the amount of criticism (Hooley et al. 1986; Vaughn and Leff 1976) and other unfulfilled aspects of affective and role behaviors (Bothwell and Weissman 1977). In addition, direct observation studies of depressed patients and their spouses indicate dysfunctional problem solving and impaired communication (Hinchliffe et al. 1975; Kahn et al. 1985).

3. *Specific physical and psychiatric disorders produce specific problems.* Although some of the problems faced by individuals and families encountering any serious illness are universal, some may be specific to a particular disorder, or to various subtypes of the disorder. Clinically, it would seem that living with depression would require different coping skills than living with chronic diabetes, arthritis, or schizophrenia. More specifically, there are several forms of depression, each with a characteristic course and outcome. The literature currently available suggests that in order to diagnose depressive disorders there is a need to understand the demographics of the illness, along with the individual's genetic heritage, history of previous episodes and life stressors, and current interactional patterns in intimate relationships. To intervene effectively, it is important to understand the impact of depression on individuals and their families and to be aware of the efficacy of available pharmacologic and psychotherapeutic treatments. For instance, although people of all ages, races and ethnic and socioeconomic levels can become depressed, statistics indicate that women are more vulnerable, particularly women who are not employed and/or are the mothers of young children (Brown and Harris 1978). Women employed outside the home are more likely to have a protective "structure" to their days as well as a diversified support network outside the family. Depressed women with young children are more likely to be dependent on their own initiative, to be isolated, and to experience extra pressure because it is almost impossible to postpone or "fake" the tasks of child rearing. This is particularly relevant in postpartum depression, which may affect as many as 20% of new mothers, with symptoms lasting 2–12 months (Hopkins et al. 1984). In any case, because depressive disorders are so prevalent among women, they are likely to have a profound impact on family life, affecting child care, marital role

performance, marital satisfaction, and overall family and child development (Coyne et al. 1987; Weissman 1979).

4. *Family members can respond to depressed patients in ways that mitigate or exacerbate symptoms and course.*

The depressed patient's interpersonal environment appears to have some influence on the onset and course of the disorder. Crucial interpersonal factors include the presence of a confidant (Brown and Brolchain 1975), the amount of criticism from relatives (Hooley et al. 1986; Vaughn and Leff 1976), and the issue of a perceived lack of interpersonal control in the marital relationship (Hinchliffe et al. 1978). Clearly, having a supportive, sustaining environment is helpful to patients, yet maintaining such a stance in the face of severe depressive symptomatology cannot be easy for family members. Providing ongoing support is likely to be particularly difficult if family members do not understand that depression is an illness. For instance, perhaps because most of the behaviors of depressed patients are not as aberrant as those of other mental illnesses, family members of depressed patients are likely to respond to symptoms differently than, for instance, family members of schizophrenic patients. Depressive symptoms are less likely to be seen as part of an illness and more likely to be seen as personality traits, "willful" behaviors, and/or reactions to actual family relationships. The impact of these perceptions can be exacerbated by the fact that one of the first symptoms of depression is often decreased libido. The resultant lack of interest in sexual activity is likely to be viewed by a spouse as evidence of marital dissatisfaction. The increased self-involvement characteristic of the disorder can further confirm a partner's insecurities or cause a child to feel neglected. Family members, for these reasons, are more likely to personalize the communications of depressed patients, feeling angry, guilty, unworthy, or unlovable as a result. In short, the interpersonal impact of the illness may be as destructive as that of psychotic disorders, and perhaps even more insidious.

It is often difficult to sort out whether marital and family problems precede depression, whether depressive illness alters perceptions of the family and marital relationships, or whether depression actually creates negative interactions. Whatever the case, over time, family members can become confused, angry, hurt, and/or frustrated in their attempts to cope. This in turn may cause them to be more critical or withdrawn from the patient, creating a feedback to the patient that may exacerbate the depression and in turn escalate family tension and conflict.

5. *Information can empower by reducing anxiety, increasing hope for change, and facilitating cognitive, affective, and behavior change.*

Depression is characterized by negative thoughts and feelings about self and others, along with hopelessness about the ability to appropriately influence others or make internal or external changes (Beck et al. 1979; Rush and Giles 1982). Negative attitudes and beliefs about self frequently correlate with negative feelings about one's spouse and/or family members, or negative evaluations of marital and family relationships (Feldman 1976; Epstein 1985; Birchler 1986).

Family researchers are currently evaluating the use of cognitive-behavior and/or strategic techniques to reduce these negative interactional sequences to help change interaction between people. The recently emerging cognitive-behavior marital therapy literature contains examples of the impact of changing cognitions on behavioral responses (Coyne 1984; Jacobson 1984a, 1984b; Weiss 1984). Key to these approaches is the idea that people's emotional responses and reactions to each other are influenced significantly by the meaning they attribute to statements or behaviors. Therapy in the cognitive-behavior model attempts to alter negative beliefs, expectations, or assumptions in order to decrease destructive interaction.

We suggest that psychoeducational workshops also can be used to shift cognitions for depressed patients and their families. This approach postulates that the provision of information and coping strategies is one way to interrupt negative interaction, providing a more positive way to interpret depressive behaviors, particularly by making it clear that depressive symptoms are part of a legitimate illness that has at least a practically predictable course and outcome. Illness can be treated, and when one family member is ill, others can be encouraged temporarily to behave in ways that decrease stress and tension.

6. *All interventions and information must be sensitive to the needs and reactions of family members.*

It is clearly very difficult to live with someone who is depressed. People react in a multitude of ways. Many family members attempt to center their lives around the patient's needs, in hopes of providing support and averting potential tragedy. Unfortunately, they often come to neglect their own needs over time. It is not surprising that people become frustrated as their energy becomes depleted and they perceive their inability to influence the patient's depression. Eventually, some family members come to feel badly about themselves and to communicate negative feelings about the patient as well. These are normal responses that would be likely during any intractable illness. However, because there is a tendency to feel guilty for negative feelings toward someone who is not well, it is important to offer support and concern while providing hope that the patient can get better and family life can improve. Suggesting that specific strategies and responses can be learned that will decrease stress encourages the expectation of change, which has been demonstrated as important in treatment outcome studies (Alexander et al. 1983; Birchler 1986; Jacobson and Margolin 1979).

7. *Applications of general principles and strategies must be tailored to an individual family in an ongoing supportive fashion.*

Every family member of a patient has experienced their own personal reaction to the changes produced by serious depression. Each usually has a personal theory of what caused the depression and what should be done to help. Simultaneously, each family member has somewhat different needs. In part, these needs depend on the depressed person's developmental stage (e.g., child, adult, elderly person) and usual role in the family (e.g., mother, homemaker, wage earner), and the characteristics of the illness (acute, recurrent, or chronic) and the additional family stressors that are present. A very common additional stress is that of psychiatric problems in other family members, as is demonstrated by assortative mating studies. As many as 60% of patients with affective disorders can be expected to be married to a spouse who is also disturbed (Merikangas 1982; Merikangas et al. 1983). Consequently, general information and general coping strategies can be useful, but they become more effective in facilitating understanding and change when they are tailored to the needs of a specific individual and specific family. For this reason, providing information without ongoing family sessions is likely to be a disservice to family members, because they may come to understand that there are ways to be more helpful without having had the chance to develop the appropriate skills to do so within their particular family.

THE PSYCHOEDUCATIONAL MODEL

Goals of the Model

The overall goal of a psychoeducational model is to improve patient and family functioning and decrease depressive symptomatology by increasing a sense of self-worth and a sense of control for both patients and families. This is accomplished by working on the following subsets of goals for patients, family members, and the family as a whole:

For the patient:
Increased sense of self-worth and self-efficacy
Increased responsibility for self and depression management
Increased ability to recognize early warning signs of relapse
Increased activity and initiative
Increased skills for coping with crises

For family members:
Increased knowledge about symptoms, treatments, and problems associated with depression
Decreased stress/worry/guilt/anger about the illness
Increased hope for change
Decreased inappropriate caretaking or functioning on behalf of the patient
Increased coping skills for managing depressive behaviors

For the family as a whole, a basic goal is to decrease tension in the family environment by modifying patient-family interactions that may be self-defeating or may perpetuate depression. This requires the establishment of a general increased sense of control through an emphasis on strengths and an increased awareness of options and choices. An increased awareness of alternatives makes each family member feel less "trapped" and thus can contribute to fewer conflicts and less stress in the family, providing a better environment in which to establish increased openness in communication.

Phases of the Model

Phase I: Connecting. The connecting phase must emphasize strengths, power, and the possibility of change for the patient and family. Clinicians must listen to each individual's perceptions of both current and past realities, being careful to validate the views presented without providing too rapid reassurance and before attempting to push anyone to change. It is crucial that clinicians demonstrate respect for the issues patients and families bring. This affirmation and validation can in part be accomplished as it is in many types of psychotherapy (i.e., by repeating back the issues: "So, if I've got this right . . ." or, "Let me see if I understand . . ."). This process of affirmation, however, must be given even more emphasis when working with depressive disorders because of the apparent importance of perceived control and because too often the patient's reality is discounted by clinicians who encourage family members to do likewise (i.e., "She doesn't really mean that, it's the depression talking," "This is a biological disorder so these specific complaints are not really relevant"). Whether or not the patient's or family's view is that of the clinician, everyone's perception of reality is important. Failing to recognize this fact only increases the likelihood of alienation before a treatment contract has been negotiated and/or makes patients and family members feel less in control than ever. Clinicians can accept a view of reality without being limited by it.

During the connecting process, clinicians should focus on strengths, emphasizing the positive attributes inherent in any situation without changing the emphasis so much as to lose credibility. Too often, when a family member is depressed, the focus for both the family and clinician becomes completely negative, i.e., on what has gone wrong. An emphasis on strengths, particularly those that relate to perceived control and choice, serves to rebalance this tendency. This type of "reframing" is not always easy to do while continuing to accept the patient's reality and should never mean a naive relabeling of troubles as blessings. In fact, sometimes it is only possible to begin by defining things as somewhat less negative, rather than as actually positive.

Gradually, the clinician can begin to focus on the relational aspects of the current situation, learning and then emphasizing how each family member fits into the picture, stressing the interrelatedness of behaviors and their ramifications. In part, this can be accomplished by gathering a history of the problem, examining attempts by family members to solve it, and finally looking at other treatments that have been tried, along with their positive or negative results. Again, it is particularly important to avoid any stimulation of blame. It is extremely difficult to live with depression, especially if it is recurrent.

Toward the end of the connecting/assessment phase, the clinician should be prepared to consolidate the information collected to present an alternative explanation of the depression and its interpersonal consequences that is more hopeful and constructive. For example, intensive marital conflict can be defined as an intense investment in each other, withdrawal as a form of protection of others, and critical comments as an attempt to help and a commitment to a better future. As with most successful reframes, redefining family members' intentions as positive or the best they could do at the time is useful in shifting negative feelings.

The final component of the connecting phase should always include the development of a contract that is based on the consolidated redefinition of the problem and the goals of treatment. The goals should depend on the degree of impairment and the number of strengths of both the patient and the family, as well as the amount of time available and the level of interest in therapeutic intervention. The contract should also involve preparation for treatment, including defining which family members are relevant to include; the duration and frequency of sessions; and the treatment methods to be used.

Phase II: The workshop. Provided early in treatment, usually during an acute episode, the workshop, which lasts 4–6 hours, emphasizes the provision of information to patients and their families, while attempting to decrease their sense of isolation and stigma. Simply seeing other reasonable people struggle with similar issues is a powerful beginning toward feeling less negative about one's own attempts to cope. The workshop is designed to have a didactic focus, but allows time for discussion and questions. Patients and family members are provided with available data about the potential causes of depression, as well as information about symptoms, course, and outcome. Characteristics of the disorder are also delineated. For instance, it is explained that unipolar depressions are likely to increase in duration and severity with age, that women are at greater risk, that recurrence is not uncommon, and that most depressions are responsive to treatment. Although it is made clear that theories of causality are only theories, the hypothesis of a combined stress–biological vulnerability model is emphasized. This concept tends to allow the patient and family to feel less critical, angry, or guilty, because it decreases the idea of personal responsibility and blame. Although "inherited" vulnerability might still be viewed as one person's responsibility, few families are immune to contributing some sort of biologic vulnerability, be it to hypertension, diabetes, or coronary artery disease. Each family member brings the possibility of some sort of tragedy to the family.

Currently available treatments are explained, along with the most recent and best available data about their efficacy. It is common for patients who suffer from serious depressions to have experienced earlier episodes and/or treatment failures. Some patients and families view psychotherapy or the use of medications as a form of personal weakness or failure. Whether psychotherapy or drug treatment is likely to be seen as the greater problem depends in part on personal and sociocultural factors. In any case, these feelings, combined with the fact that many patients may have been seen by poorly trained clinicians or tried on less than therapeutic doses or inappropriate drugs, can contribute to resistance to treatment or hopelessness about change. Family members and patients who are skeptical about the effectiveness of therapy or the possibility of change may be encouraged by hearing the most recent research findings and/or information about what constitutes an adequate trial of any treatment. It is particularly important for those who are severely depressed, i.e., those for whom drugs appear to be the most effective form of intervention (Elkin et al. 1986), to understand the advantages of medication. It is important, however, to understand the basic assumptions of the particular participants in the workshop when explaining the range of possible interventions.

Finally, specific information about the reciprocal impact of depression and family life is outlined, along with suggestions and strategies designed to aid family members in coping more effectively with depression. (See Table 1 for an outline of topics.)

The theme of the coping section of the workshop concentrates on interrupting negative or nonproductive sequences of interaction between depressed patients and their significant others. This is accomplished in part by acknowledging the difficulty of living with depression for both patients and families, especially having to deal with a lack of energy, interest, and enthusiasm for life. To help manage these symptoms, workshop leaders emphasize the importance of the patient continuing to function (at least at a minimal level) even when initiative is low, the importance of the family not overhelping or infantilizing the patient, and, finally, the importance of clear unambiguous communications and realistic feedback. These themes and the educational material developed from them are based on the work of those with a systems orientation, such as Coyne (1976), and a cognitive orientation, such as Beck et al. (1979).

Our workshops for families of patients with schizophrenia did not include the patient. Because they were held early in treatment and the patient was often still acutely psychotic, it was felt that the patient could not tolerate the need to concentrate and participate for such an extended period. This is less of a problem for patients with depression, most of whom are not psychotic and are treated on an ambulatory basis. Such patients can attend to the material presented in the workshop and are often eager to hear the information. Those patients with delusional depressions or severe retarded depressions do have difficulty with a workshop or group format during the acute episode, and it is usually advisable to wait until they have partially recovered before including them in sessions of this sort. In the psychoeducational program we provided for our inpatient unit, we found it was possible to include even these patients after a few weeks of treatment.

It is our experience that family members participate differently when the patient is present—they are somewhat less likely to talk about the burdens imposed by the illness and the frustrations they feel as a result. This chance to ventilate is important, yet its value must be weighed against the value of having the entire family hear the same information together, a process that lays the groundwork for working with less inhibition and overprotection in ongoing sessions on these issues. One group at our institute met this challenge by dividing the workshop in half, devoting the morning session to information for the full group and the afternoon to separate sessions

Table 1. Outline of topics for patient-family psychoeducational sessions on depression

---

I. Defining depression
  A. Definitions and descriptions of depression and mania
  B. How depression differs from "the blues" we all experience (length of time it lasts, impact on mood, functioning, self-esteem, responsiveness to the environment)
  C. Possible causes: the stress-vulnerability model
    1. Genetic factors
    2. Biochemical factors
    3. Life events, stresses, and family problems

II. Depression and the interpersonal environment
  A. What depression looks like: interpersonal difficulties
    1. Oversensitivity and self-preoccupation
    2. Unresponsiveness (to reassurance, support, feedback, sympathy)
    3. Behaviors that appear willful
    4. Apparent lack of caring for others, unrealistic expectations
    5. Apparent increased need to control relationships
    6. Inability to function at normal roles, tasks
  B. Negative interactional sequences
    1. Family attempts to help: coax, reassure, protect (potential for overinvolvement)
    2. Patient is unresponsive, family escalates attempts to help or withdraws
    3. Patient feels alienated, family becomes withdrawn, angry, or both
    4. Family feels guilty and returns to overprotective stance
    5. Patient feels unworthy, hopeless, infantilized
    6. Families burn out over time but remain caught in guilt/anger dilemma
    7. Alienation and/or overprotection

III. Treatments
  A. Psychotropic medication
  B. Psychotherapies
  C. Other treatments

Table 1. Outline of topics for patient-family psychoeducational sessions on depression—Continued

IV. Coping with depression
- A. What to avoid
  1. Too rapid reassurance
  2. Taking comments literally
  3. Attempting to be constantly available and positive
  4. Allowing the disorder to dominate family life
- B. Creating a balance (neither over- nor underresponsive)
  1. Recognition of multiple realities
  2. Distinguishing between the patient and the disorder
  3. Decreasing expectations temporarily
  4. Providing realistic support and reinforcement
  5. Avoiding unnecessary criticism (but providing feedback when necessary)
  6. Communicating clearly and simply (proverbially)
  7. Providing activity, structure
- C. Taking care of self and family members other than the patient; skills for self-preservation
  1. Time out (away from patient)
  2. Avoiding martyrdom
  3. Accepting own negative feelings
  4. Minimizing the impact of the disorder
- D. Coping with special problems
  1. Suicide threats and attempts
  2. Medication
  3. Hospitalization
  4. Atypical responses

Note. An earlier version of this table was published in Anderson CM, Griffin S, Rossi A, et al: A comparative study of the impact of education vs. process groups for families of patients with affective disorders. Fam Process 25:192, 1986. Copyright 1986 by Family Process, Inc. Reprinted with permission.

for patients and families (Frank and Kupfer 1986). The ongoing work was not family oriented, so the "groundwork" issue was less significant.

The response to all informational sessions, whether they were provided in day-long or half-day–long workshops or in a series of weekly sessions, has always been extremely positive. Patients and families were grateful for the information and perhaps even more grateful for the new collaborative relationship these sessions established with professionals, a collaboration that demonstrated increased respect and equality.

Phase III: Application and maintenance in ongoing treatment. We live in a culture that provides daily examples that information alone does not change behavior. There are few smokers who do not know smoking causes lung cancer; few errant dieters who do not know the impact of high-calorie desserts. It is unrealistic to assume that information alone can solve the problems inherent in or caused by depression and/or to assume that change occurs easily and quickly. Although it is not clear how many marriages were troubled before one spouse became depressed, certainly there is evidence that marital problems remain after depressive symptoms have abated (Bothwell and Weissman 1977; Paykel et al. 1969; Weissman and Klerman 1972; Hinchliffe et al. 1975). It is likely that parent-child problems also linger. For these reasons, the original treatment contract must include the possibility of ongoing family sessions. The length and frequency of these sessions can be modified dependent on the needs of the individuals involved in a particular situation.

The focus of ongoing sessions then is the application of the principles and themes of the workshop. The initial goal is simply to begin to live with the symptoms of depression without allowing them to totally dominate family life. Because of the decreased energy involved, it may be necessary to work out some sort of temporary relief from household and child-care responsibilities. If the spouse, extended family, or paid help step in, it is important to find ways to maintain the depressed individual's sense of worth by emphasizing the illness factor and the temporary nature of these arrangements. Even during this time, the importance of maintaining an established structure and some level of activity must be stressed. If it is a child or adolescent who has been depressed, the crucial issue is to avoid undue negative influence on the normal tasks of the life cycle by continuing to allow small steps toward emancipation.

For the patient, the secondary goals of ongoing treatment include the prevention of future episodes through early identification, stress reduction, and the provision of ongoing support. For family members, the goal is also stress reduction. Part of the art of this therapy is helping family members to be supportive of the patient without encouraging them to become overinvolved and thus infantilizing the patient and decreasing their own energy and coping resources over time. Discussing this dilemma directly sometimes helps to make patients less reactive as family members set some limits on the amount of support they can provide.

As the patient's symptoms abate, it is often possible to work on relationship issues that constitute ongoing stresses that may act as triggers of depressive episodes. Although it is questionable just how much can be done for severely dysfunctional marriages, it is certainly possible to decrease stress in relationships that are basically sound or moderately impaired. In part, this may depend on the length of time and satisfaction in the marriage before the onset of symptoms. Commitment to a marital relationship is likely to be stronger if there has been time to accumulate a number of good memories before the impact of any catastrophe, including that of serious depression.

As the depressed person begins to have more energy and initiative, very often it is necessary to address the need for a rebalance of power and a reworking of issues of intimacy in marital or family relationships. In a marriage, it is crucial not to pressure either the depressed individual or the spouse to attempt to develop more intimacy than they can handle comfortably. Many individuals, not just those who are depressed, feel they *should* want more intimacy than they have and thus pressure and/or blame themselves or their partner when this is not easily forthcoming. In any case, relationship "fine-tuning" should only be done after the acute phase of the illness has passed and the patient is functioning reasonably normally.

As the depression lifts, the patient and family members must be helped to modulate their expanding expectations of one another. Too often, problems have been attributed to depression and everyone comes to believe that once "it" is over, relationships and family life will be happy and conflict free. Problems that existed before the depression will no doubt continue, and certainly many problems are inherent in family life. Ongoing education about the nature of "normal" family relationships can help to keep expectations at a reasonable level.

SPECIAL APPLICATIONS

The context and focus of psychoeducational sessions vary depending on the age, sex, family position, and life cycle stage of the patient and the family. Most of this chapter has assumed that the patient is a young or middle-aged adult with a marital partner; however, it has become increasingly clear that children, adolescents, and the elderly also experience significant depressive disorders, and that their parents, siblings, and/or adult children also need help to deal with these problems effectively.

Children and Adolescents

The diagnosis of depression in children and adolescents is not without controversy. Until very recently, there has been a reluctance by clinicians to diagnose children and adolescents as depressed. The psychoanalytic view maintained that children and adolescents were cognitively incapable of developing a depression and terms such as "masked depression" or "depressive equivalent" were used when describing behavioral and emotional symptoms (Orvaschel et al. 1980). Psychiatric symptoms in children and adolescents were often defined as transitory phenomena without major prognostic significance. Follow-up studies recently summarized by Ryan and Puig-Antich (1986) have failed to support the view that serious child and adolescent psychopathology will usually remit of its own accord. There are indications that certain disorders will continue or reoccur in adulthood. The belief held by families and clinicians alike that benign neglect is sufficient for the problems of children and adolescents appears to be unfounded. [Editor's note: For a more detailed discussion of depression in children and the impact of parental depression on the child, see Chapters 4 and 5.]

In 1980, the authors of DSM-III took the position that the diagnostic criteria for affective disorders in adults was valid for other age groups including children, adolescents, and the elderly. Variations exist in the frequency of symptoms in different age groups but not in symptom criteria. The prevalence of depressive disorders in children and adolescents is unclear; however, there is some evidence that 1–2% of children (Kashani et al. 1983) and 2–4% of adolescents meet criteria (Kashani et al. 1987). As with adults, recurrence is very common (Kovacs et al. 1984a, 1984b).

Involving the family in the assessment and treatment of children and adolescents is essential to gaining an understanding of the presence and severity of depression symptoms and disorders. Often family members can provide information that is unavailable from the child who may not understand the questions, may be unable to adequately articulate responses, or may be unaware of the frequency or duration of behaviors. Family members can also provide information regarding family stress factors, history of psychiatric illness in relatives, or family interactional problems.

A psychoeducational model for children or adolescents can be similar to that used with adults. The basic assumptions hold, as do the phases: connecting, information giving, and ongoing interventions. Families with a depressed child or adolescent appear to be a demographically and structurally heterogeneous group. As with most forms of therapeutic intervention, the precipitant of requests for assessment is highly relevant in determining the initial needs of families. These families may present asking for help with a crisis, such as a suicide attempt, or with more chronic difficulties, such as long-standing withdrawal or underachievement. In many cases, parents are aware that their child is depressed and define it as such. However, because parents tend to be less aware of a child's thoughts and feelings and much more aware of the overt behavioral manifestations of depression (i.e., loss of friends, declining school performance, increased negative or abusive interactions with parents or sibling), it is often the secondary complications of a child's depression that cause a request for help. In these cases, the child may be defined as lazy, bad, manipulative, mean, or withholding, because most adults, including the parents, only see negativistic, frustrated, or withdrawn behavior. It is not unusual for these children to describe their parents as disappointed with or angry at them. Often parents are. Frequently these attitudes toward the child appear to develop in response to depressive features, whereas in other cases, negative attributions and interactions were present long before the child developed a depression, perhaps as part of a parent's own symptomatology.

It is likely that a family history of psychiatric illness will be reported. There is evidence that a family history positive for affective disorder is more common for depressed children, particularly when the child's depression is chronic with no clear-cut precipitant (Orvaschel et al. 1980). There is also evidence for increased incidence of alcoholism and anxiety disorders among these parents (Puig-Antich et al. 1985; Strober 1984). Consequently, the families of these children and adolescents are likely to be multiproblem and require an unusually sensitive connecting process. In this process, it is important to recognize that most parents feel responsible for their children and thus feel guilty if there is something wrong. Therapeutic efforts must be made to reduce both guilt and anxiety. The use of positive reframes to define ways in which parents have tried to help their children (even if the effects have been unsuccessful) is crucial.

The workshop format has been useful in helping families with depressed children. It is generally advisable to structure workshops for parents of prepubertal children and parents of adolescents separately because the normal developmental tasks of each group are different and the types of coping strategies and appropriate parental responses suggested are also geared toward age-appropriate norms. Typically, workshops for adolescents and parents include sessions together as well as separate meetings for groups of parents and teenagers alone. Workshops related to depressed children are usually offered for parents alone.

Much of the same information regarding symptomatology in adult patients is relevant for children and adolescents, with the major difference being the prevalence of specific symptoms for different age groups. For example, a recent study suggests that dysthymic and major depressive syndromes are as frequent in prepuberty as in adolescence (Kovacs et al. 1984a, 1984b). However, prepubertal children show more frequent depressive appearance, physical complaints, separation anxiety, and agitation, whereas adolescents have hopelessness, appetite impairment, weight loss, phobias with avoidance, and sleep disturbance (Ryan and Puig-Antich 1986). Parents must be provided with information that will help them to expect and cope with these symptoms—information and skills that specifically take into account the child's concurrent needs for nurturance or protection and developing autonomy.

Some of the typical questions from parents who attend the child-oriented workshop involve how much to monitor children, particularly those who have made suicide gestures or attempts; how to differentiate normal problems from symptoms of an illness; how much to question children regarding their mood, or how much to share parental feelings or concerns with the child or adolescent; whether to protect the child or adolescent from distressing information; how to handle child and particularly adolescent resistance to treatment; how to set limits that are neither too restrictive nor too lax; how to deal with the process of recovery that ebbs and flows; and how to learn signals that indicate early warning signs of relapse.

The application phase of the model must attempt to help parents to neither underreact nor overreact to the disorder, to sort out other family problems or issues that increase family stress levels, and to foster both the recovery process and the ongoing developmental tasks and needs of the depressed child without neglecting the needs of other children in the family or the parents themselves.

The Elderly

Loss is frequently associated with the onset of a depressive episode, and, for the elderly, loss is a frequent and ongoing experience. The loss of health, loss of career and income, and the death of friends, relatives, or spouse all create stress that for some can precipitate a serious depression. In addition to increased vulnerability due to loss, the elderly are at greater risk to develop depression secondary to illnesses or as the result of side effects from medications used to treat medical problems more common to older adults. It is estimated that 15–20% of the population 65 years and older suffer from depressive disorders (Papolos and Papolos 1987).

One of the major differences between this age group and their younger cohorts is the likelihood that depression will present in the form of complaints about physical health. This, in conjunction with the frequent difficulty of differentiating between depression and dementia, can lead to delays or even failure to provide treatment for many of these patients. After a diagnosis of depression, the family members who are most likely to be involved in the treatment of elderly patients are spouses, adult children, and siblings. There is relatively little difference in the application of the model for this group, with the exception of a greater focus on the relationship of physical illness and medications to depression, and an explanation of medical tests and procedures that are more frequently necessary.

As with families of depressed children and younger adults, clinicians must address the need for a support system for the patient and other family members. In the elderly population, it is not unusual to find the nondepressed spouse overtaxed by the caretaking responsibilities that have become necessary during the illness. The physical and emotional strain that might have been easier to cope with during earlier life stages may prove overwhelming for an aging husband or wife. Helping spouses to think about their own needs is important, although it is not uncommon that they are reluctant to allow outside professionals or organizations to help and in some cases are reluctant to "burden" adult children. Finding ways that increase the likelihood that the spouse will use resources is important.

Children of elderly depressed patients face their own struggles, which may include coming to terms (perhaps precipitously as the result of the depression) with a parent-child role reversal. It may be the first time that they must contend with the need to take care of a parent who has taken care of them. Attitudes, fears, and confusion can interfere with children being able to offer an appropriate level of support. During the workshop phase, it is helpful to discuss common responses of adult children, including a tendency toward increased distance from parents who are less functional; overly controlling attitudes and behaviors as a result of discomfort in taking on any authority at all vis-à-vis a parent; or overly helpful responses that can make the parent feel increasingly useless, deepening the sense of expendability that elderly people often experience.

In the ongoing treatment phase, it becomes particularly important to identify those attitudes or fears that inhibit adult children from being a resource. Stress and problems in their own personal, marital, or work lives can be an issue, as can unresolved problems between themselves and their parents. For some, the crisis may be an opportunity to improve a relationship that was previously strained. Encouragement in staying connected and not retaliating with anger or withdrawal may aid these adults in pursuing this opportunity and/or avoiding regrets when their parent is gone.

SUMMARY AND CONCLUSIONS

Despite evidence that family factors appear to influence onset, course, and treatment outcome in depression, few treatment programs have been developed that address the needs of family members or attempt to involve them in treatment. Based on the positive response to our psychoeducational program for schizophrenia, we have attempted to design a program that applies similar principles and methods to the treatment of depression. This chapter has described the rationale, goals, and content of a workshop for depressed patients and their families. The entire program is based on the assumption that a biologic/genetic vulnerability to depression interacts with environmental stresses to produce symptoms of depression. It proposes to help patients and family members by sharing information on etiology, phenomenology, and effective coping skills, in the context of providing ongoing support and help in the implementation of this material to the problems of everyday family life. It is assumed, in turn, that this process will decrease family stress, increase effective coping, and improve relationships between family members and with members of the treatment team.

The key, of course, is not simply to teach family members to be better caretakers, i.e., to be less critical or more supportive of the patient. Such an approach would place increased stress on family members over time, resulting in "burnout" or exhaustion. Family members cannot and should not be trained to provide a "perfect" environment without any of the stresses and conflicts inherent in normal family life. Rather, it is important to understand just what the depressed person does that elicits criticism or what about living with depression makes it difficult to provide ongoing support. Only by looking at the needs and problems of each individual can we develop interventions that are effective in interrupting the negative interactional sequences that are disturbing to all family members.

Although some attempts have been made to examine the impact of the workshop (Anderson et al. 1986a), no attempts have been made to investigate the entire program in a comprehensive way or to perform a controlled clinical trial to determine the effectiveness of psychoeducational treatment for depression. Nevertheless, family members and patients have been exceedingly positive in their feedback about the process. Studies of the efficacy of this form of treatment with depressed patients are indicated.

In addition to issues of treatment outcome, this form of family intervention has implications for the training of family therapists. Most family models of treatment are based on systemic principles and imply that a knowledge of systems theory is necessary and sufficient to treat almost all problems presented. This model suggests that undersanding family systems is necessary but not sufficient. Understanding specific disorders, including possible etiologies, range of symptoms, available treatment options, and biopsychosocial implications is vital in helping families.

REFERENCES

Alexander JF, Barton D, Waldron H, et al: Beyond the technology of family therapy: the anatomy of intervention model, in Advances in Clinical Behavior Therapy. Edited by Craig KD, McMahon RJ. New York Brunner/Mazel, 1983, pp 48–73

American Psychiatric Association: Diagnostic and Statistical Manual of Mental Disorders, 3rd Edition. Washington, DC, American Psychiatric Association, 1980

Anderson CM, Reiss D: Psychoeducational family approaches. Paper presented at the annual meeting of the American Psychiatric Association, Los Angeles, CA, May 1984

Anderson C, Hogarty G, Reiss D: Family treatment of adult schizophrenic patients: a psychoeducational approach. Schizophr Bull 6:490–505, 1980

Anderson CM, Griffin S, Rossi A, et al: A comparative study of the impact of education vs. process groups for families of patients with affective disorders. Fam Process 25:185–206, 1986a

Anderson CM, Reiss D, Hogarty G: Schizophrenia and the Family. New York, Guilford Press, 1986b

Anisman H, Zacharko RM: Depression: the predisposing influence of stress. Behavioral and Brain Sciences 55:89–137, 1982

Beardslee WR, Bemporad J, Keller MB, et al: Children of parents with major affective disorder: a review. Am J Psychiatry 140:825–832, 1983

Beck AT, Rush AJ, Shaw BF, et al: Cognitive Therapy of Depression. New York, Guilford Press, 1979

Bertelsen A, Harvald B, Hange M: A Danish twin study of manic-depressive disorders. Br J Psychiatry 130:330–351, 1977

Birchler GR: Alleviating depression with marital therapy. Journal of Psychotherapy and Family 2:101–116, 1986

Bothwell S, Weissman M: Social impairments four years after an acute depressive episode. Am J Orthopsychiatry 47:231–237, 1977

Boyd J, Weissman M: Epidemiology of affective disorders: a re-examination and future directions. Arch Gen Psychiatry 38:1039–1046, 1981

Briscoe CW, Smith JB: Depression and marital turmoil. Arch Gen Psychiatry 29:811–817, 1973

Brown GW, Brolchain MW: Social class and psychiatric disturbance among women in an urban population. Sociology 9:225–254, 1975

Brown GW, Harris TO: Social origins of depression: a study of psychiatric disorders in women. New York, Lee Press, 1978

Brown GW, Harris T, Copeland JR: Depression and loss. Br J Psychiatry 130:1–18, 1972

Carroll BJ, Feinberg M, Greden JF, et al: A specific laboratory test for the diagnosis of melancholia: standardization, validation, and clinical utility. Arch Gen Psychiatry 38:15–22, 1981

Charney DS, Menker DB: Receptor sensitivity and the mechanism of action of antidepressant treatment: implications for the etiology and therapy of depression. Arch Gen Psychiatry 38:1160–1175, 1981

Collins J, Kreitman N, Nelson B, et al: Neurosis and marital interaction, III: family roles and functions. Br J Psychiatry 119:233–242, 1971

Coyne JC: Depression and the response of others. J Abnorm Psychol 85:186–193, 1976

Coyne JC: Strategic therapy with married depressed persons: initial agenda, themes and interventions. Journal of Marital and Family Therapy 10:53–62, 1984

Coyne JC: Strategic marital therapy for depression, in Clinical Handbook of Marital Therapy. Edited by Jacobson NS, Gurman AS. New York, Guilford Press, 1986, pp 495–511

Coyne JC, Kessler RC, Tal M, et al: Living with a depressed person. J Consult Clin Psychol 55:347–352, 1987

Elkin I, Shea T, Watkins J, et al: NIMH Collaborative Research Program: General effectiveness of treatment. Paper presented at the meeting of the Society for Psychotherapy Research, Wellesley, MA, June 1986

Falloon IR, Boyd JL, McGill CW, et al: Family management in the prevention of exacerbations of schizophrenia. N Engl J Med 306:1437–1440, 1982

Feldman LB: Depression and marital interaction. Fam Process 15:389–395, 1976

Frank E, Kupfer D: Psychotherapeutic approaches to treatment of recurrent unipolar depression: work in progress. Psychopharmacol Bull 22:525–563, 1986

Goldstein M, Kopeikin H: Short and long term effects of combining drug and family therapy, in New Developments in Interventions With Families of Schizophrenics. Edited by Goldstein MD. San Francisco, CA, Jossey-Bass, 1981

Hammen CL, Peters SD: Interpersonal consequences of depression: responses to men and women enacting a depressed role. J Abnorm Psychol 87:322–332, 1978

Hinchliffe M, Hooper D, Roberts FJ, et al: A study of the interaction between depressed patients and their spouses. Br J Psychiatry 126:164–172, 1975

Hinchliffe MK, Hooper D, Roberts FJ: The melancholy marriage: depression in marriage and psychosocial approaches to therapy. New York, Wiley, 1978

Hogarty GE, Anderson CM, Reiss DJ, et al: Family psychoeducation, social skills training and maintenance chemotherapy in the aftercare treatment of schizophrenia. Arch Gen Psychiatry 43:633–642, 1986

Hogarty GE, Anderson CM, Reiss DJ: Family psychoeducation, social skills training, and medication in schizophrenia: the long and short of it. Psychopharmacol Bull 23:12–13, 1987

Hooley JM, Orley J, Teasday JD: Levels of expressed emotion and relapse in depressed patients. Br J Psychiatry 148:642–647, 1986

Hopkins J, Marcus M, Campbell S: Postpartum depression: a critical review. Psychol Bull 25:498–515, 1984

Jacobson NS: Marital therapy and the cognitive behavioral treatment of depression. Behavior Therapist 7:143–147, 1984a

Jacobson NS: The modification of cognitive processes in behavior marital therapy: integrating cognitive behavioral intervention strategies, in Marital Interaction: Analysis and Modification. Edited by Hahlweg K, Jacobson NS. New York, Guilford Press, 1984b, pp 285–307

Jacobson NS, Margolin G: Marital therapy: strategies based on social learning and behavioral exchange principles. New York, Brunner/Mazel, 1979

Kahn J, Coyne JC, Margolin G: Depression and marital conflict: the social construction of despair. Journal of Social and Personal Relationships 2:447–462, 1985

Kashani JH, McGee RO, Clarkson SE, et al: Depression in a sample of 9-year-old children. Arch Gen Psychiatry 40:1217–1233, 1983

Kashani JH, Carlson GA, Beck NC, et al: Depression, depressive symptoms, and depressed mood among a community sample of adolescents. Am J Psychiatry 144:931–934, 1987

Kidd KK, Egeland JA, Molthan L, et al: Amish study, IV: genetic linkage study of pedigrees of bipolar probands. Am J Psychiatry 141:1042–1048, 1984

Klerman GL, Weissman MM, Rounsaville BJ, et al: Interpersonal psychotherapy of depression. New York, Basic Books, 1984

Kovacs M, Feinberg TL, Crouse-Novak MA, et al: Depressive disorders in childhood, I: longitudinal prospective study of characteristics and recovery. Arch Gen Psychiatry 41:219–239, 1984a

Kovacs M, Feinberg TL, Crouse-Novak MA, et al: Depressive disorders in childhood, II: a longitudinal study of the risk for a subsequent major depression. Arch Gen Psychiatry 41:643–649, 1984b

Kupfer DJ, Spiker DG, Rossi A, et al: Recent diagnostic and treatment advances in REM sleep and depression, in Treatment of Depression: Old Controversies and New Approaches. Edited by Clayton PJ, Barrett JE. New York, Raven Press, 1983, pp 31–52

Leff J, Vaughn C: The role of maintenance therapy and relatives' expressed emotion in relapse of schizophrenia: a two year follow-up. Br J Psychiatry 139:102–104, 1981

McLean PD, Hakistan AR: Clinical depression: comparative efficacy of outpatient treatments. J Consult Clin Psychol 47:818–836, 1979

Merikangas KR: Assortative mating for psychiatric disorders and psychological traits. Arch Gen Psychiatry 39:1173–1180, 1982

Merikangas KR, Bromet EJ, Spiker DG: The relationship of assortative mating to social adjustment and course of illness in primary affective disorder. Arch Gen Psychiatry 40:795–800, 1983

Merikangas KR, Prusoff B, Kupfer D, et al: Marital adjustment in major depression. J Affective Disord 9:5–11, 1985

Orvaschel H, Weissman MM, Kidd KK: Children and depression—the children of depressed parents; the childhood of depressed patients; depression in children. J Affective Disord 2:1–16, 1980

Papolos DF: The psychoeducational approach to major affective disorders. Paper presented at the meeting of the American Family Therapy Association, New York, June 1984

Papolos DF, Papolos J: Overcoming Depression. New York, Harper & Row, 1987

Paykel ES, Myers JK, Dienelt MN, et al: Life events and depression: a controlled study. Arch Gen Psychiatry 21:753–760, 1969

Post RM, Ballenger JC (eds): Neurobiology of Mood Disorders. Baltimore, Williams and Wilkins, 1984

Puig-Antich J, Luken E, Davies M, et al: Psychosocial functioning in prepubertal major depressive disorders, II: interpersonal relationships after sustained recovery from affective episode. Arch Gen Psychiatry 42:511–517, 1985

Rounsaville BJ, Prusoff BA, Weissman MM: The course of marital disputes in depressed women: a 48-month follow-up study. Compr Psychiatry 21:111–118, 1980

Ryan D, Puig-Antich J: Affective illness in adolescence, in Psychiatry Update: American Psychiatric Association Annual Review, Vol 5. Edited by Frances AJ, Hales RE. Washington, DC, American Psychiatric Press, 1986

Rush AJ, Giles DE: Cognitive therapy: theory and research, in Short Term Psychotherapies for Depression. Edited by Rush AJ. New York, Guilford Press, 1982, pp 143–174

Rush AJ, Beck AT, Kovacs M, et al: Comparative efficacy of cognitive therapy and imipramine in the treatment of depressed outpatients. Cognitive Therapy and Research 1:17–37, 1977

Schlesser MA, Altshuler KZ: The genetics of affective disorder: data, theory, and clinical applications. Hosp Community Psychiatry 34:415–422, 1983

Seligman M, Abramson L, Semmel A, et al: Depressive attributional style. J Abnorm Psychol 88:242–247, 1979

Shaw B: A comparison of cognitive therapy and behavior therapy in the treatment of depression. J Consult Clin Psychol 45:543–551, 1977

Strober M: Familial aspects of depressive disorders in early adolescence, in Current Perspectives on Major Depressive Disorders in Children. Edited by Weller EB, Weller RA. Washington, DC, American Psychiatric Press, 1984

Vaughn CE, Leff JP: Influence of family and social factors on the course of psychiatric illness. Br J Psychiatry 129:125–127, 1976

Weiss RL: Cognitive and strategic interventions in behavioral marital therapy, in Marital Interaction: Analysis and Modification. Edited by Hahlweg K, Jacobson NS. New York, Guilford Press, 1984, pp 337–355

Weissman M: The depressed woman: recent research. Social Work 19:25, 1972

Weissman MM: The psychological treatment of depression: evidence for the efficacy of psychotherapy alone, in comparison with and in combination with pharmacotherapy. Arch Gen Psychiatry 36:1261–1269, 1979

Weissman MM, Akiskal HS: The role of psychotherapy in chronic depression: a proposal. Compr Psychiatry 25:23–31, 1984

Weissman MM, Klerman GL: Sex differences and the epidemiology of depression. Arch Gen Psychiatry 34:90–111, 1972

Weissman MM, Paykel ES: The Depressed Woman: A Study of Social Relationships. Chicago, IL, University of Chicago Press, 1974

Widmer RB, Codoret RJ, North CS: Depression in family practice: some effects on spouses and children. J Fam Pract 10:45–51, 1980

Winokur G, Behar D, Van Valkenburg C: Is a familial definition of depression both feasible and valid? J Nerv Ment Dis 166:764–768, 1978

Chapter 9

Depression and Families: A Comment

Myrna M. Weissman, Ph.D.

Chapter 9

Depression and Families: A Comment

There is overwhelming evidence from clinical, family, epidemiologic, and pedigree studies that depression is a family affair. The risk of depression is markedly increased in the relatives of patients with depression. This risk extends to the adult first-degree biological relatives (i.e., parents and siblings) as well as to the children and adolescents.

The findings showing that the children of depressed parents are at high risk for psychiatric disorders including depression have been confirmed now by at least five studies of children using the DSM-III criteria and direct interviews of children. Additionally, these studies show that assortative mating is high, that depressed patients tend to marry depressed or psychiatrically ill spouses, and that when this occurs the risk to children for major depression, as well as other behavioral problems, is accelerated. The high-risk studies cannot sort out whether genetic factors are involved in the transmission of psychiatric disorders between patients and relatives. Recent studies of extended pedigrees in the older Amish and in several Israeli kindred suggest that genetic factors are undoubtedly important for bipolar disorder. Their role in major depression is less clear.

The work by Keitner and associates from the Brown group shows the persistence of impaired family functioning in the acute phase of a depressive illness as well as in the recovery period. Although some improvement in family functioning in the resolution of the depression is reported, family problems were still perceived as present by the

---

This research was supported in part by Grant MH-36197 from the Affective and Anxiety Disorders Research Branch, National Institute of Mental Health, Rockville, Maryland. This work was also supported in part by the John D. and Catherine T. MacArthur Foundation Mental Health Research Network on Risk and Protective Factors in the Major Mental Disorders.

families with depressed members. Importantly, they have shown the relationship between the duration of the episode and the impairment in family functioning. These findings suggest that rapid alleviation of the symptoms may have some impact on reducing family impairment.

The work by Beardslee, Klerman, and Keller, from Harvard and Cornell, extends the findings from the studies of children of depressed patients to a randomly selected sample of children drawn from a community health plan. Again, the study shows the impact on a child of having an affectively ill parent, and the persistence of the findings to nonpsychiatric samples.

The contributions by Glick and by Jacobson and their associates are efforts to develop interventions dealing directly with the family issues. The approaches are varied, including family therapy in hospitalized severely ill patients as well as marital and cognitive therapy in conjoint or individual format. Clearly, these studies emphasize the importance of developing the spectrum of interventions.

The familial nature of depression and its serious impact on family functioning are sturdy findings. Interpretation as to etiology or mechanisms, however, varies widely. A sociologist might emphasize the social consequences of living in a family in which there is a depressed parent. Inadequate social supports or role models may be the mechanism for transmission of the disorders between the generations. The psychologist might emphasize the learning of attributional styles or the attachment losses suffered by children nurtured by a depressed parent. The work of Coyne graphically demonstrates these mechanisms. An epidemiologist would view depression in a family member as a risk factor for depression in other family members. This might lead to further questions as to whether this risk factor extended to all family members in proximity to the depressed relative (as in a contagious disease) or only to the biological relatives, whether or not in proximity to the depressed proband (as in a genetic or biological disorder). A geneticist would be interested in determining the pattern and modes of transmission among the biological first- and second-degree relatives of the depressed person. The clinician faced with troubled families will not be able to await the resolution of these ideological debates, but will look for clues in the data for effective treatment and prevention of further illness.

The familial nature of depression has direct clinical and research implications, even in the absence of understanding etiology. Clinically, the findings suggest that the treatment of depression must be done in a family context. A family perspective has been traditional in psychiatric practice. The data suggest that there needs to be an extension of the family perspective. The perspective should include information not only on the relatives who are in direct contact with the patient, as is commonly obtained in clinical practice, but also on the biological relatives, whether or not in contact with the patient, and whether alive or dead. A detailed inquiry into the psychiatric status of first- and possibly second-degree relatives of the patient, including children, can yield important information of potential value for diagnoses as well as for possible prevention. Moreover, a mental health professional treating a depressed parent should make direct inquiry into the psychiatric status of the children. Because there is often great discrepancy between the child's and the parents' report of the child's psychiatric status, direct interviews with the children, especially adolescents, are important (Weissman, in press). Alternatively, the mental health professional, educator, etc., treating children should inquire directly about the psychiatric status of the parents. Treatment of a parent's depression may have an impact on the health of the child.

The emerging data also argue against an exclusive family systems view of depression, which sees the depressed patient's symptoms as a way of manipulating the family. The data show that depression runs in families, regardless of whether the biological relatives are in direct contact or are having a social impact on the patient. The data also suggest that family or couples therapists, because of the high degree of familial aggregation and assortative mating, should make direct and systematic inquiry into the psychiatric status of the family member and not just into the family member's perception of the patient's psychiatric status.

Systematic collections of the patient's pedigrees along with family history information on the relatives and direct psychiatric assessments, when indicated, should become standard in psychiatric evaluation. These methods are relatively easy to learn and can be readily adapted to clinical practice. (See Swift 1987 and Baker et al. 1987 for a discussion.)

In terms of research, there is now considerable evidence for the familial nature of affective disorders. There is still very little information on the efficacy of treatment of depressed children and adolescents. Clinical trials aimed at understanding the efficacy of the various treatments of adults who are depressed and their applicability to younger ages are needed. These studies should begin with testing the treatments in individuals before moving to a family, conjoint, or group context.

In summary, the data emphasize the importance of parental and family depression as risk factors for various health problems and depression in relatives. There are many treatments now available, including pharmacotherapy and psychotherapy, whose efficacy has been established through well-designed clinical trials. Direct inquiry into the past and current psychiatric status of the patient, as well as the patient's biological family members and children, may be a first step toward early identification of depression and treatment intervention.

REFERENCES

American Psychiatric Association: Diagnostic and Statistical Manual of Mental Disorders, 3rd Edition. Washington, DC, American Psychiatric Association, 1980

Baker NJ, Berry SL, Adler LE: Family diagnoses missed on a clinical inpatient service. Am J Psychiatry 144:630–632, 1987

Swift M: The family history in clinical psychiatric practice. Am J Psychiatry 144:5, 1987

Weissman MM: Psychopathology in the children of depressed parents: direct interview studies, in Relatives at Risk for Mental Disorders. Edited by Dunner DL, Gershon ES. New York, Raven Press (in press)